Robyn Keynes and Theatre In Heights in association with Neil
McPherson for the Finborough Theatre presents

A Finborough Theatre co

The European premiere

VELOCITY
by **Daniel Macdonald**

FINBOROUGH | THEATRE

First performed at Persephone Theatre, Saskatoon, SK, Canada:
Wednesday, 16 February 2011

First performance at the Finborough Theatre: Sunday, 27 April 2014

VELOCITY
by **Daniel Macdonald**

Cast in order of appearance

Dot	**Rosie Day**
Laura	**Helene Wilson**
Michael	**Nicholas Cass-Beggs**
Zoo	**Sion Alun Davies**
Ming	**Siu-See Hung**
Jee	**Waleed Akhtar**

The performance lasts approximately 90 minutes.

There will be no interval.

Director	**Blythe Stewart**
Designer	**Ella-Marie Fowler**
Lighting Designer	**Petr Vocka**
Stage Manager	**Charlie Risius**
Producer	**Robyn Keynes**

Our patrons are respectfully reminded that, in this intimate theatre, any noise such as rustling programmes, talking or the ringing of mobile phones may distract the actors and your fellow audience-members.

Waleed Akhtar | Jee

Theatre includes *The Kite Runner* (Nottingham Playhouse and Liverpool Playhouse), *Betrayed* (Tron Theatre, Glasgow), *Under 11's* (Soho Theatre), *Black I* (Kali Theatre and Ovalhouse), *Love Match* (Everyman Theatre, Cheltenham), *I Call My Brothers* (Arcola Theatre), *A Midsummer Night's Dream* (Tooting Arts Club), *Masculine Law* (Big Chill Festival and Tara Arts), *Hearts and Minds* (National Tour), *Screwface* (Tristan Bates Theatre), *Gladiator Games* (ETC, Germany) and *Thoughts and Truths* (Old Red Lion Theatre).

Film includes *Salmon Fishing in the Yemen, Sidney, Sparks and Embers, Lipstikka* and *Diary of a Jihadi*.

Television includes *Law and Order UK, Doctors, Edge of Heaven* and *Dustbin Baby*.

Nicholas Cass-Beggs | Michael

Trained at the Oxford School of Drama. Theatre includes *La Fille du Régiment, Tamerlano, The Rake's Progress, Orlando* (Royal Opera House, Covent Garden), *The Zero Hour* (West Yorkshire Playhouse and National Tour), *Carousel* (Barbican, Théâtre du Châtelet, Paris, and The Lowry, Manchester), *6 Degrees* (Contact Theatre, Manchester and National Tour), *Antigone* (Royal Exchange Theatre, Manchester), *The Snowman* (Peacock Theatre and Korean Tour), *The Temperamentals* (Greenwich Theatre), *The Lion, the Witch and the Wardrobe* (New Vic Theatre, Staffordshire), *Ménage à Trois* (Cochrane Theatre), *Park Avenue* (Lilian Baylis Theatre), *Pajama Game* (Union Theatre), *Kismet* (English National Opera at the London Coliseum) and *Trailer* (Camden People's Theatre).

Contemporary dance includes five years as a soloist with Ballet Theatre Munich from 1997-2002 and three years with Ballett Nordhausen from 1994-1997. Nicholas has performed in works choreographed by Kim Brandstrup, Mark Bruce, Philip Taylor, Jiri Kylian, Rui Horta, Jonathon Lunn, Stefan Haufe and Henning Paar.

Sion Alun Davies | Zoo
Trained at the Guildhall School of Music and Drama.
Theatre includes *Pen-Blwydd Poenus Pete* (Theatr Iolo), *Outside On The Street* (Arcola Theatre), *A Marked Man* (HighTide Festival Theatre), *A Soldier and a Maker* (Barbican Theatre) and *Festopia* (Theatre503).
Television includes *Doctors* and *Treflan*.

Rosie Day | Dot
Theatre includes *Les Misérables* (Palace Theatre), *The Winter's Tale, The Playboy of the Western World, Summerfolk* (National Theatre), *The Pussy Riots, Spur of the Moment* (Royal Court Theatre) and *Microwave* (National Theatre Studio).
Film includes *The Seasoning House* for which she won Best Actress award at the Fantaspoa Film Festival 2013 and was named *Screen International* Star of Tomorrow, the BAFTA nominated *Good Night, Ironclad: Battle for Blood, Sixteen, Heart of Lightness* and *Soror.*
Television includes *Siblings, Misfits, Homefront, DCI Banks, Harley Street, My Life as a Popat, Fallen Angel, The Romantics, Bernard's Watch, Darwin's Daughter, Family Affairs, Big Train, Indeep, Black Books* and *Hope and Glory.*

Siu-See Hung | Ming
Trained at Arts Educational Schools.
Theatre includes *Love* (Southwark Playhouse), *Something There That's Missing* (Theatre503), *Nic Knight's Tales* (Park Theatre), *Granny Dumpling, Ba Banh It* (Yellow Earth Theatre at The Albany), *Dim Sum Nights, Theef* (Yellow Earth Theatre) and *Our Town* (King's Head Theatre).

Helene Wilson | Laura
Theatre includes *The Seven Year Itch* (Queen's Theatre), *Aunt Dan and Lemon* (Almeida Theatre), *Life During Wartime* (Lyric Theatre), *Navy Pier* (Soho Theatre) and *Since You Left Us* (Tristan Bates Theatre).
Film includes *The Dark Knight, Hellboy, Down, Caught Out, Horses for Courses* and *Virgin Birth.*
Television includes *Relentless, The Other Wife, Inside Waco, Body Story 2, Rosemary and Thyme* and *Survivors.*

Daniel Macdonald | Playwright

Playwright Daniel Macdonald makes his professional UK debut with this production of *Velocity*. He is an award-winning playwright, teacher and director. Most recently, his play *A History of Breathing* received its world premiere at Persephone Theatre in Saskatoon and was shortlisted for the national Carol Bolt Award. It is published by Playwrights Canada Press. Other plays include *Pageant, MacGregor's Hard Ice Cream and Gas, Mercy, Radiant Boy* and *Johnny Zed The Musical! (The Musical)*. His film series *Redemption, SK* was televised in Canada and nominated for a Canadian Independent Series Award. As a teacher, Daniel has co-written several plays with and for high school students including *Blind Love* which was performed at the 2013 Edinburgh Festival. He is a recipient of the Enbridge National PlayRites award (Alberta Theatre Projects), a two-time recipient of the City of Regina Writer's Award, and a two-time recipient of the SMPIA award for acting. He continues to teach high school and university classes, and splits his time between Saskatchewan and Prince Edward Island.

Velocity was originally workshopped at the Saskatchewan Spring Festival of New Plays and had its world premiere at Persephone Theatre, Saskatoon, directed by Del Surjik in February 2011. It won the New Works of Merit playwriting competition in New York City, and received its US premiere with Twilight Theatre at the HERE Space in New York City in 2012. It was also seen as part of the LARK Play Development Centre's Playwrights' Festival in New York City.

Blythe Stewart | Director

Productions at the Finborough Theatre include the staged reading of Bekah Brunstetter's *A Long and Happy Life* for *Vibrant 2013 – A Festival of Finborough Playwrights*. Direction includes *Julie and Paul* (LOST Theatre), *Game* (Ovalhouse), *There's No Place Like Home* (Etcetera Theatre), the UK premiere of Kerrigan and Lowdermilk's musical *Party Worth Crashing* (Edinburgh Festival) and the European premiere of *Tallgrass Gothic* (Site-specific for Theatre In Heights). She is a recipient of the Amelia Hall Gold Medal Scholarship, and has studied and worked internationally from Toronto to London to Moscow as a director, writer and assistant director. She has a Masters in Theatre Directing from East 15 Acting School and studied at the National Academy of Dramatic Arts (GITIS) in Moscow.

Upcoming productions include a European premiere of Canadian play *East of Berlin* at the Southwark Playhouse in June/July 2014.

Ella-Marie Fowler | Designer
Ella-Marie Fowler graduated from Wimbledon College of
Art, University of the Arts London, with First Class Honours
in 2011. Designs include include *Days of Hope* (Rose and
Crown Theatre), *East London Dance: 25 Years and Counting...*
(Stratford Circus), *The Merchant of Venice* (Brockley Jack
Theatre) and *Strung* (Collisions Festival at The Central School
of Speech and Drama), and When I Say Jump's award-winning
production *A Modern Town* (Pleasance Theatre, London and
Pleasance Courtyard, Edinburgh). In 2013, she was selected
to represent the Royal Opera House, Covent Garden, and
East London Dance as an Emerging Artist, collaborating with
choreographer Botis Seva and composer Alex Groves to create
a scratch performance for the Linbury Studio, Royal Opera
House, Covent Garden. She strives to practice environmentally
sustainable methods within her work.

Petr Vocka | Lighting Designer
Trained at RADA in Postgraduate Diploma in Stage Electrics
and Lighting Design. Lighting Designs include *Phaedra's Love*
and *Mercury Fur* (Gielgud Theatre at RADA), *New Electric
Ballroom, Love and Money, M.Butterfly* and *Son Et Lumiere*
(GBS Theatre at RADA). He has also been Video Designer for
Betrayal (GBS Theatre) and *All's Well that Ends Well* (Jerwood
Vanbrugh Theatre at RADA) and Technical Stage Manager
including relighting *How to be Immortal* (National Tour).

Robyn Keynes | Producer
Trained on the Acting and Contemporary Theatre course
at East 15 and The Optimists programme, run by China
Plate. Freelance producing includes *Kitty Litter* (theSpace,
Edinburgh, and Courtyard Theatre, London), *A Modern Town*
(Pleasance London and Pleasance Courtyard, Edinburgh).
. She was Assistant Producer at Independent Productions
in 2012/2013, working on the sell-out UK tours of *Boy In A
Dress* and *The Bear* (co-production with Improbable). She was
Festival Coordinator of the National Student Drama Festival
2014. She has just started working at commercial producers
Smith and Brant through the Stage One Apprenticeship
Scheme. Her passion lies strongly in new writing and aims
to bring bold, original work to both the commercial and
subsidised sectors.

Production Acknowledgements
Briar Stewart, Kate Costello, Muireann Bird, Collie McCarthy, Leon Rubin, Mary Jane Macdonald, Melanie Rogoskwi, Eva Mann, Leonie Zeumer, Aiste Gramantaite, Ruth O'Dowd, Leo Wood, Lauren Bowles, Workspace, Eloise Tomlinson.

FINBOROUGH | THEATRE
VIBRANT **NEW WRITING** | UNIQUE **REDISCOVERIES**

'Audacious and successful... West London's Finborough Theatre is one of the best in the entire world. Its programme of new writing and obscure rediscoveries remains "jaw-droppingly good"'. Time Out

'A disproportionately valuable component of the London theatre ecology. Its programme combines new writing and revivals, in selections intelligent and audacious.' Financial Times

'The tiny but mighty Finborough...one of the best batting averages of any London company' Ben Brantley, The New York Times

'The Finborough Theatre, under the artistic direction of Neil McPherson, has been earning a place on the must-visit list with its eclectic, smartly curated slate of new works and neglected masterpieces' Vogue

Founded in 1980, the multi-award-winning Finborough Theatre presents plays and music theatre, concentrated exclusively on vibrant new writing and unique rediscoveries from the 19th and 20th centuries. Behind the scenes, we continue to discover and develop a new generation of theatre makers – through our Literary team, and our programmes for both interns and Resident Assistant Directors.

Despite remaining completely unsubsidised, the Finborough Theatre has an unparalleled track record of attracting the finest creative talent who go on to become leading voices in British theatre. Under Artistic Director Neil McPherson, it has discovered some of the UK's most exciting new playwrights including Laura Wade,

James Graham, Mike Bartlett, Sarah Grochala, Jack Thorne, Simon Vinnicombe, Alexandra Wood, Al Smith, Nicholas de Jongh and Anders Lustgarten; and directors including Blanche McIntyre.

Artists working at the theatre in the 1980s included Clive Barker, Rory Bremner, Nica Burns, Kathy Burke, Ken Campbell, Jane Horrocks and Claire Dowie. In the 1990s, the Finborough Theatre first became known for new writing including Naomi Wallace's first play *The War Boys*; Rachel Weisz in David Farr's *Neville Southall's Washbag*; four plays by Anthony Neilson including *Penetrator* and *The Censor*, both of which transferred to the Royal Court Theatre; and new plays by Richard Bean, Lucinda Coxon, David Eldridge, Tony Marchant and Mark Ravenhill. New writing development included the premieres of modern classics such as Mark Ravenhill's *Shopping and F***ing*, Conor McPherson's *This Lime Tree Bower*, Naomi Wallace's *Slaughter City* and Martin McDonagh's *The Pillowman*.

Since 2000, new British plays have included Laura Wade's London debut *Young Emma*, commissioned for the Finborough Theatre; two one-woman shows by Miranda Hart; James Graham's *Albert's Boy* with Victor Spinetti; Sarah Grochala's *S27*; Peter Nichols' *Lingua Franca*, which transferred Off-Broadway; and West End transfers for Joy Wilkinson's *Fair*; Nicholas de Jongh's *Plague Over England*; and Jack Thorne's *Fanny and Faggot*. The late Miriam Karlin made her last stage appearance in *Many Roads to Paradise* in 2008. UK premieres of foreign plays have included Brad Fraser's *Wolfboy*; Lanford Wilson's *Sympathetic Magic*; Larry Kramer's *The Destiny of Me*; Tennessee Williams' *Something Cloudy, Something Clear*; the English premiere of Robert McLellan's Scots language classic, *Jamie the Saxt*; and three West End transfers – Frank McGuinness' *Gates of Gold* with William Gaunt and John Bennett; Joe DiPietro's *F***ing Men*; and Craig Higginson's *Dream of the Dog* with Dame Janet Suzman.

Rediscoveries of neglected work – most commissioned by the Finborough Theatre – have included the first London revivals of Rolf Hochhuth's *Soldiers* and *The Representative*; both parts of Keith Dewhurst's *Lark Rise to Candleford*; *The Women's War*, an evening of original suffragette plays; *Etta Jenks* with Clarke Peters and Daniela Nardini; Noël Coward's first play, *The Rat Trap*; Charles Wood's *Jingo* with Susannah Harker; Emlyn Williams' *Accolade*; Lennox Robinson's *Drama at Inish* with Celia Imrie and Paul O'Grady; John Van Druten's *London Wall* which transferred to St James' Theatre; and J. B. Priestley's *Cornelius* which transferred to a sell out Off Broadway run in New York City.

Music Theatre has included the new (premieres from Grant Olding, Charles Miller, Michael John LaChuisa, Adam Guettel, Andrew Lippa, Paul Scott Goodman, and Adam Gwon's *Ordinary Days* which transferred to the West End) and the old (the UK premiere of Rodgers and Hammerstein's *State Fair* which also transferred to the West End), and the acclaimed 'Celebrating British Music Theatre' series, reviving forgotten British musicals.

The Finborough Theatre won *The Stage* Fringe Theatre of the Year Award in 2011, *London Theatre Reviews'* Empty Space Peter Brook Award in 2010 and 2012, the Empty Space Peter Brook Award's Dan Crawford Pub Theatre Award in 2005 and 2008, the Empty Space Peter Brook Mark Marvin Award in 2004, and swept the board with eight awards at the 2012 OffWestEnd Awards including Best Artistic Director and Best Director for the second year running. *Accolade* was named Best Fringe Show of 2011 by *Time Out*. It is the only unsubsidised theatre ever to be awarded the Pearson Playwriting Award (now the Channel 4 Playwrights Scheme) nine times. Three bursary holders (Laura Wade, James Graham and Anders Lustgarten) have also won the Catherine Johnson Award for Pearson Best Play.

www.finboroughtheatre.co.uk

The Finborough Theatre has the support of the Channel 4 Playwrights' Scheme, sponsored by Channel 4 Television and supported by The Peggy Ramsay Foundation

The Finborough Theatre is a member of the Independent Theatre Council, Musical Theatre Network UK and The Earl's Court Society www.earlscourtsociety.org.uk

Mailing
Email admin@finboroughtheatre.co.uk or give your details to our Box Office staff to join our free email list. If you would like to be sent a free season leaflet every three months, just include your postal address and postcode

Follow Us Online
 www.facebook.com/FinboroughTheatre
www.twitter.com/finborough

Feedback
We welcome your comments, complaints and suggestions. Write to Finborough Theatre, 118 Finborough Road, London SW10 9ED or email us at admin@finboroughtheatre.co.uk

Playscripts
Many of the Finborough Theatre's plays have been published and are on sale from our website.

Finborough Theatre T-Shirts are now on sale from the Box Office, available in Small and Medium £7.00.

Smoking is not permitted in the auditorium and the use of cameras and recording equipment is strictly prohibited.

In accordance with the requirements of the Royal Borough of Kensington and Chelsea:

1. The public may leave at the end of the performance by all doors and such doors must at that time be kept open.

2. All gangways, corridors, staircases and external passageways intended for exit shall be left entirely free from obstruction whether permanent or temporary.

3. Persons shall not be permitted to stand or sit in any of the gangways intercepting the seating or to sit in any of the other gangways.

The Finborough Theatre is licensed by the Royal Borough of Kensington and Chelsea to The Steam Industry, a registered charity and a company limited by guarantee. Registered in England and Wales no. 3448268. Registered Charity no. 1071304. Registered Office: 118 Finborough Road, London SW10 9ED.

The Steam Industry is under the overall Artistic Direction of Phil Willmott. www.philwillmott.co.uk

Daniel Macdonald

VELOCITY

OBERON BOOKS
LONDON

WWW.OBERONBOOKS.COM

First published in 2014 by Oberon Books Ltd
521 Caledonian Road, London N7 9RH
Tel: +44 (0) 20 7607 3637 / Fax: +44 (0) 20 7607 3629
e-mail: info@oberonbooks.com
www.oberonbooks.com

A catalogue record for this book is available from the British
Library.

PB ISBN: 978-1-78319-147-5
E ISBN: 978-1-78319-646-3

Cover image: Eloise Tomlinson

Printed and bound in Great Britain by
Marston Book Services Limited, Oxfordshire

Visit www.oberonbooks.com to read more about all our books
and to buy them. You will also find features, author interviews and
news of any author events, and you can sign up for e-newsletters
so that you're always first to hear about our new releases.

Acknowledgements

Del Surjik
Sturgis Warner
Ben Henderson
Heather Inglis
The Lark Play Development Center (New York),
Saskatchewan Playwrights Centre Persephone Theatre
(Saskatoon), Colleen Murphy, Mary Blackstone,
The Regina Playwrights Circle, The University Of Regina,
Melanie Rogowski, Averie Macdonald, Ivan Anderson

Velocity received its world premiere at Persephone Theatre in Saskatoon, Saskatchewan, Canada featuring the following cast and crew:

Dot	*Jamie Lee Shebelski*
Ming	*Stephanie Sy*
Zoo	*Jeremy Walmsley*
Jee	*Sanjay Narine*
Laura	*Kristina Agosti*
Michael	*Matthew Burgess*

Director	Del Surjik
Assistant Director	Kristen Holfeuer
Set and Costume Designer	Carla Orosz
Lighting Designer	Byron Hnatiuk
Stage Manager	Laura Kennedy

Characters

DOT

15 years old

MING

15 years old – of Asian descent

ZOO

17 or so – White

JEE

18-20 – Appears to be of South Asian
or Middle Eastern descent

LAURA

Dot's mom – early forties

MICHAEL

Dot's dad – similar age to Laura – perhaps a bit older

*The audience is entering. Occasionally during this (pre-show) time
DOT, 15, appears and re-appears, looking around the space as though
getting things ready. She is perky, fun, stylish. She has her phone out and
occasionally checks it or sends texts. She chats with the audience as they
enter. (Note: This is an entirely flexible pre-show routine.)*

*She looks at the audience and smiles, nervous but confident. She pauses,
catches her breath and steps off stage to return with an easel with large
paper and a large marker. Carefully, she places the marker on the easel
and looks at it for a moment, pondering, making sure that everything's
right. Exits. She returns with a stylish tote bag from which she extracts
a small pad and pen. DOT does not need to have the bag all the time
during the play but at various times it is used to hold items like phones,
makeup, etc. It is not the same as the purse that MING has later. DOT
looks at her easel and then her audience and scribbles some information
in her notebook as she glances at the audience.*

Lights fade to black.

*When the lights come up a man and woman are in the middle of breakfast.
These are DOT's parents, well-groomed and attractive. They are in a sort
of "movement piece"; a dance. It is the "Dance of the Morning Breakfast".
They neither appear to be comfortable in the dance nor do they appear to
be controlling it. It is as though they are puppets going through repetitive,
pedestrian "modern dance" movements like sipping coffee, looking in
the fridge, eating toast, fixing their tie, putting on makeup in a tiny,
confined space. They occupy only a few square feet. LAURA, the mother,
at times seems to be looking for something. They move about each other
fluidly but awkwardly. They continue to do all this during the upcoming
chat with DOT.*

*DOT returns and watches them for a moment, then has an idea and takes
out her phone and snaps a picture of them.*

*(Note on images: They should be large (for the audience) and appear
instantaneously with DOT snapping the picture. They are never entirely
compatible with the image we see on stage. They last 3-4 seconds and
fade.)*

Image #1: A candid shot of Dot's parents in
the kitchen; Heads turned, eyes wide. Mom is
adjusting an earring. Dad has jam on his face.

Immediately we see it projected somewhere. DOT looks at the pic and laughs and then puts the phone away. The projected pic disappears.

LAURA picks up her purse from the floor and roots through it searching for something. MICHAEL is oblivious, eating. Finally, in frustration LAURA goes into her husband's pocket and extracts a cell phone and dials. DOT writes in her notepad. Satisfied, she looks at the audience.

DOT: *(To audience.)* Good evening. Before I start –

A phone rings inside her bag. She takes it out, answers. It's her mom. During this conversation they do not look at each other. LAURA continues to be engaged in a dance with MICHAEL.

DOT: Hello?

LAURA: Why am I calling my number and you're answering my phone?

DOT: Shit. I took your phone by accident. I'm so sorry Mom.

LAURA: Where's your phone?

DOT: I have it.

LAURA: So you have both phones. Great. Fantastic.

DOT: I'm sorry, Mom. They look identical.

MICHAEL begins to look for something.

DOT: Whose phone do you have?

LAURA: Your father's.

DOT: He hasn't left?

LAURA: He's looking for his lunch. When can I get my phone?

DOT: I'm bringing his lunch. *(To audience.)* At this point I should probably introduce –

MICHAEL grabs the phone from his wife.

MICHAEL: Dot, where's my lunch?

DOT: I'm bringing your lunch.

MICHAEL: Where?

DOT: To work. I want us to have lunch.

MICHAEL: That's sweet. Where's your mother's phone?

DOT: I have my mother's phone.

MICHAEL: Where are you?

DOT: I'm here. Busy. With the audience. Getting ready.

LAURA grabs the phone back from MICHAEL.

LAURA: You get over here right now.

MICHAEL: *(Yelling at the phone.)* Dot, you get over here right now.

LAURA: I'm sorry, honey but I can't be at your thing today. Your presentation.

DOT: Ha. Ha. Very funny. You're part of my presentation.

LAURA: Well I can't be. I'm meeting with your father.

DOT: It's too late, Mom, my thing's going to be fucking fantastic.

LAURA: Dot, please don't say that.

DOT: It's going to be fantastic.

LAURA: I'm sure it is.

DOT: Mom, you have no choice. You'll have to just meet with him now.

LAURA: Don't be silly. We're having breakfast.

MICHAEL: What did she say?

LAURA: Meet with you now. *(MICHAEL scoffs.)* And I can't pick you up later.

DOT: Mom, what did I just say?

MICHAEL: *(Yelling into the phone that LAURA's holding.)* When are you bringing my lunch?

DOT: At lunch time.

LAURA: *(To MICHAEL.)* At lunch time.

MICHAEL: When? I have a busy day.

DOT: So, Mom, you're giving me a ride home. After my thing.

LAURA: No. Your father is.

DOT: Uh…I don't think so.

LAURA: I thought you said he was going to be at your thing.

DOT: He is. I just…I'm not sure if he'll be able to like, drive.

MICHAEL: What did she say?

LAURA: You are.

MICHAEL: I am what?

LAURA: Going to be at her thing.

MICHAEL: No, I'm not. I told you I'm not.

LAURA: She says you are.

MICHAEL: Well I'm not. Don't tell her I am.

LAURA: You told her you are.

MICHAEL: I didn't tell her – *(MICHAEL grabs the phone from LAURA.)* Sweetie, I can't be at your thing today.

DOT: Yes, you can. You are. Mom too. *(Pause. DOT hears something.)* Hang on. I have another call. *(They quietly continue to dance.)*

She goes into her bag and extracts her own phone and looks at it. She smiles and puts it to her ear. She now holds a cellphone at each ear. Her parents go to darkness.

DOT: Hey Zoo.

ZOO appears at a distance. He is in shadow, a half-here, half-not figure, he has a jacket on covering bulk. He has a phone to his ear. He does not see DOT; she does not see him. She waits. He does not respond.

DOT: Hey Zoo.

…

Zoo?

…

Zoo? You ok? What's up?

Zoo?

ZOO presses his cellphone off and lowers the phone. He disappears.

DOT looks at her phone and ponders a moment. She's brought back by her parents on the other phone. Quickly she puts her phone away and goes back to her mom's phone. Her parents reappear.

MICHAEL: Dot!

LAURA: Dot!

DOT: What!

MICHAEL: Dot. You're really not listening. I have a big meeting with Bill today.

DOT: Screw the meeting with Bill, Dad.

MICHAEL: I can't "screw" the meeting with Bill. We have a major deal we're trying to put together. Huge!

LAURA: Did she say "screw"?

DOT: It's ok. You won't let me down. You'll see. You're already perfect.

LAURA: *(Yells into MICHAEL's phone.)* You watch your mouth young lady. Screw.

MICHAEL: *(To LAURA.)* She has no idea what this deal means.

LAURA: Ask her when I can get my phone.

MICHAEL: Can't. Have to go. I'll be late.

MICHAEL pockets his phone, single-pecks his wife on the cheek, picks up a briefcase and exits.

LAURA realizes she has no phone. She turns to her daughter. There's an awkward moment. LAURA wants to walk over to her daughter but for some reason, can't. They stand there looking at each other across a massive chasm. DOT puts the phone away.

LAURA: So when is all this over?

DOT: I'm not sure. It shouldn't take – Oh shit. I forgot. I have to tutor my friend.

LAURA: Don't say shit, Dot. Shit is such an ugly word. Your friend.

DOT: Yeah. She asked for some help. Are you nervous, Mom?

LAURA: A little. Just a little.

DOT: You'll be fine. They'll love you. Like I do.

LAURA: I can't believe I don't have my fucking phone.

DOT: Don't worry, Mom. I'll get it to you when you really need it.

LAURA: Dot, we need to talk later. There are…things I need to tell you.

DOT: Ok. That's good. I have things too.

LAURA walks away and sits in a swivel chair in darkness and waits.

DOT: If I'm going to execute this assignment – this project – properly, there are several things…people that need introduction before we get started. One. My mom. This is my mom. She's very busy –

DOT moves to where her mother is sitting. DOT rolls her mother in the swivel chair into position. They look at each other. DOT nods at her. LAURA begins. The lights come up on LAURA in her swivel chair. She focuses in, smiling as though suddenly a camera is on her.

LAURA: *(Laughing.)* Thanks Gary. Hi everybody and welcome. This week I'd like to talk about interesting, important parts of your body. Those parts that perhaps don't get the kind of attention they deserve. Today I want to talk to you about your hips, ladies. Your hips. Grab them. Grab your hips. At home. Right now. That's right. Stand up and grab them. How do they feel to you? Do they feel like they're yours? Foreign? Alien? Are they warm or cold? Fat or thin? Don't lie, now. Have they fallen? Expanded? Firmed? Do they take you to hell or heaven? Here's a question. How do they feel when your man grabs a hold of them? Are they worth hanging on to? How many children have you had pass through those hips? One? Twelve? Did you reclaim those hips after childbirth? Or did they tell the rest of your body to go to hell and explode all over you? Because, let me tell you something. Nothing defines a woman more than her hips. Nothing. Not her eyes, her hair, her breasts, her feet.

So hold them. And love them. Even if no one else will. Because…they are your centre. Your soul. Be very good to them. Later in the hour we'll be looking at the history of hips, / *(DOT begins to speak to the audience here. LAURA begins to fade in volume and into the darkness even as DOT resumes focus.)* why they've gone out of style and what we can do to bring them back. Because they're here aren't they, ladies? They're attached to all of us. And they ain't goin' nowhere. All right. Just a reminder that Laura's Lessons are brought to you by the good people at Oasis tanning and beauty spas. There are three in the metro area open 8:00 am to 10:00 pm daily. We'll be back after this.

Towards the end of the overlap, DOT comes and gets LAURA and begins to roll her off even as LAURA continues to speak but becomes almost inaudible.

DOT: My mom has a big thing today. It's very important to her. They may make her a host. A host of the TV morning show. It's like the number three morning show in the city, but still. That would be, like, amazing. For her. Right now she just makes guest appearances where she talks mostly about important things. To her. Like, you know, the shape of her daily declining body. Only she makes you believe that it's your body that's, like, declining. She's very good. They want her to audition. For host. Today. She's got a busy day.

LAURA is gone. DOT assumes centre. Immediately MING enters rolling a bed complete with plush, stuffed dolls right up to DOT. She jumps on it, lays down on her back and looks at a teen magazine and reads from it. She looks to DOT for permission to begin speaking.

DOT: *(Quietly.)* Ok.

MING: "You already know he's a dream, now discover if he's into you" *(She looks up.)* Seriously?

DOT: *(DOT joins her on the bed.)* They work. I'm telling you.

MING: "You're at school and your locker is jammed and you're late for phys ed class. He…A) tells you he wishes he could help but he and the guys have a free period and they're going to get Frappacinos, B) offers to take you to the office, C) acts as your own personal rescue squad, D) calls a teacher for help and leaves.

DOT: *(To audience.)* This is Ming. *(MING waves. DOT takes a picture of her.)*

IMAGE #2: Ming's class photo. Perfection in every way. Right down to her school uniform.

DOT: Ming is perfection. She walks, talks, breathes, sleeps, eats as though each moment has been divinely orchestrated by a god. As you can see, she is vaguely Asian which adds to the allure. Ming's my best friend.

MING: *(Flipping pages.)* Does foreplay have anything to do with foreskin?

DOT: *(A carefree laugh.)* This is why I like Ming so much. In fact if I didn't know any better, I would think that Ming was me. A better, happier, nicer, more innocent me. As long as Ming is with me, I feel complete. I don't let her out of my site.

MING: I like this purse. *(In the mag. She shows it to DOT.)*

DOT: Oh yeah. I bought it.

MING: You did?

DOT: Yeah. It looks exactly like the one in that video. You know, the one with the girl who looks all…everything. Hot and beautiful and she's on that street shopping? And every time she comes out of a store, she's singing a different verse and she has a different outfit on. I think it's the third time she comes out and all her friends are following her and they turn on to the street and the cars are stopped and the guys are checking them all out from the side walk. And she gives her girls a look…kind of…like that? *(Gives a look.)* And the girls all nod, like "we know what you're talkin about" and they all break into this dance, like right on the street. It's really cool cause all the girls are on the

street, dancing like this hip hop kind of thing but not?
Like post-hip-hop? And the guys – like their jaws are just
dropping now, right? Because, they're just stupid guys and
they didn't think the girls had it this much together. And
then the guys start dancing with them and the girls, like,
shake their asses at the guys and the guys are all like…
(She smiles and grinds while on the bed.) and the girls are all
wearing those little shorts and the guys don't have their
shirts on…and the girl – oh shit I can't remember her
name – she's new – anyway, the camera comes right up to
her – like closeup – and it follows her hand which is like,
at first – on her face and she's touching her face and hair –
like this – *(She does.)* while the other hand is going down all
– like – over her body, like she's caressing her body *(DOT
is.)* like she's turned on by all the people and the street and
the money and then we see everybody else and they're all
doing it too, like writhing and touching themselves only
it's in a big organized, like V, like vortex of writhing and
touching in the middle of the street and the guys are doing
something different. They're more like doing this *(She
tries to imitate a male sexuality.)* and the girls are more like
this *(Girl sexual move – the shift in her movements from child
to sexual object is jarring, stark, disturbing.)*, and suddenly
it's nighttime on the same street there's like a million
people and cop cars and flashing lights – like the world has
stopped for her – have you seen that video?…

MING: I…I don't…

DOT: …And in the end she throws the purse in the air and
there's, like this close-up of the purse up in the air and all
the money falls out of it in slow motion all over everything
like rain in the nighttime. I love that video. So I went out
and bought it. The purse. So, you like the purse?

MING: Yeah.

DOT: You want it?

MING: *(Pause.)* Kay.

DOT: Maybe sometime we can go out and you can wear it.

MING: Yeah. Maybe.

The pulse of techno music is heard. From across the stage, lights flash in a very specific spot revealing two young men, gyrating very closely together to the music. Their movements are controlled, serious, intense. They are ZOO and JEE. ZOO is white. JEE appears to be of South Asian descent. Unless otherwise indicated ZOO and JEE always appear in the same way – under pulsating light – and doing the same thing – dancing together – or at least very near each other – in similar style each time – not over the top. From time to time ZOO gets too close to JEE when they dance and always seems a little too eager and out of place. DOT sees the boys, squeals and steps away from the bed to watch them for a moment and then turns to the audience. MING disappears with the bed.

DOT: I love young men. I know no one else does. They are crass, ignorant. They emit more sounds and odors from their bodies than a horny baboon. They project the strength of Kong when they actually possess the power of a ladybug. They are incomprehensible. They dress and eat like they are homeless, laugh and speak like they are disabled. I love them because they are so willing to love me. Completely and unconditionally if I so much as breathe in their direction. They want to touch and be touched, kiss and be kissed, hold and be held. Their greatest love and fear is for their own bodies. It is a great and terrible thing to them and they worship it in hundreds of wonderful, perverse ways.

She looks to them and nods, then as they approach she snaps a picture.

ZOO: Your body.

JEE: My body.

ZOO: Their body.

JEE: Her body.

ZOO: His body.

JEE: Everybody.

ZOO: Loves some body.

The boys continue to dance for a bit. ZOO gets a little too close to JEE and JEE shoves him away.

ZOO: Sorry. *(ZOO breaks away from the dance and goes to DOT while JEE continues to dance on his own.)*

JEE: *(Sotto voce.)* Zoo!

ZOO: It's ok. *(He is standing in front of DOT. DOT's slightly annoyed.)* Hey, Dot.

DOT: Zoo, what did we say?

ZOO: Yeah, but I just wanted –

The conversation overlaps big-time. It should seem a little incoherent.

DOT:
K. But it's gotta be quick, K?
(DOT's trying to stay pleasant.) ZOO:
I…I know, I just was like –

DOT:
…Cause we…like

ZOO:
It's good to like, uh…

DOT:
I know, Zoo. ZOO:
…See you…and uh –

DOT:
Oh. You too, Zooey. For realz.
Like that's fine but – ZOO:
…So, I like…uh – I wanted
to ask you about
Your experiment.
I think I can –

DOT:
Zoo. Ok. But maybe, like not now,
You know?

ZOO:
Oh. Oh yeah. So later, ok, yeah.

DOT:

    Yeah. Oh yeah. Later.
    But right now –

                    ZOO:

                    I know, I know. I just…uh…
                    was nervous and uh…

He heads back to where JEE is dancing and dances with him for a moment. JEE and ZOO exchange a laugh. The lights and music fade. They're gone. MING has gone with the bed, leaving DOT standing centre stage. DOT is slightly apologetic.

DOT: That's Zoo and Jee. Um…more on them later. OK. One thing you should know. Don't listen to any of these people if they try to tell you shit. This is my experiment. Everyone is here for a specific reason. And you are my audience. I can already tell you like Zoo and Jee. Don't. They'll fuck you up every time. Oh. And I know this is supposed to be a school presentation and everything but I will be saying the word "fuck" on several occasions.

Are we ready? Oh. I almost forgot. The guest of honour. My dad. *(Thinks.)* Screw it. You'll get to know him shortly. Let's just start.

She moves her gaze from one section of the audience to the other.

No one has to go pee or anything? *(Pause.)* Ok. Good. Just remember one thing. 6 5 4 3 2 1…zero. Ok? Just imagine. Your entire world in six seconds.

We start at the top.

She steps back over to where her easel is. She takes out her phone (as a watch), looks at it, looks back at the audience, braces herself and takes a deep breath…

…Six!

The lights go to black and there is the sound of a huge explosion and a flash. The lights come up on MICHAEL, falling. MICHAEL twists and writhes in the air. Initially DOT seems like circus ring-master.

MICHAEL: *(He is freaking out loudly.)* Shit!… Holy fuck! What the –

DOT: *(To audience.)* My father.

Somewhere during this conversation DOT takes out her phone and takes a picture.

Image #3: Dad falling. Surprised look. Office
tower above in the background. Glass spraying.

MICHAEL: I'm…I'm falling!

DOT: 73 stories.

MICHAEL: From my office!

DOT: I know! Your beautiful, comfortable office! Corner,
with plush leather for a chair and a lovely secretary, more
efficient than ants on a caterpillar.

MICHAEL: My plate glass window…

DOT: With a view on the world as spectacular as chocolate
fudge.

MICHAEL: Shattered –

DOT: Into…into 15 thousand tiny pieces from a tremendous
explosion from within your mahogany desk.

MICHAEL: Blasted –

DOT: Straight out along with the desk, unshatterable glass, and
a photo of –

MICHAEL: *(He is seeing it as it falls beside him.)* My wife and
daughter –

DOT: Somersaulting by his head like a family of trapeze artists.
We all fall like hailstones about to smash into the gawking
parade of spectators down below. With Dad attempting to
linger for a moment at the 73rd floor. 73 stories above the
street, still alive…

MICHAEL: My feet…legs!

DOT: Flailing like a…cyclist…

*DOT is excited and attempts to illustrate on her easel as she speaks.
She is drawing a crude, cheap diagram of the "high diving act".*

…Like those old Coyote-Road-Runner movies. Like Wile
E. Coyote trying to dash back to the edge of his cliff. Like
Yosemite Sam… "I came here to see the high-divin act and
I'm a gonna see the high divin act." He's hoping for a fall

but he's the one who falls. Every time. He wants someone else to fall. He wants Bugs to fall but Bugs doesn't. Ever. Yosemite Sam does. And when he falls, there's a moment when he pauses and looks straight out, then his feet drop, then his body, then his head, then his ears. And he's looking straight out the whole time. At us. Like, "What the fuck just happened here?" Then, when it seems as though he's all gone, he reaches back up and grabs his hat cause he left without it. Not the Coyote. Yosemite Sam. Coyote doesn't have a hat.

MICHAEL: *(To DOT.)* Dot! What the hell's going on!?

DOT: You're falling.

MICHAEL: I don't have time! I was in the middle –

DOT: – Well, you are. 73 stories. I'm here to do an experiment. *(DOT takes a look at him through binoculars.)*

MICHAEL: Dot, I told you. I can't be involved in your little science class project. *(Speed-dials on his cell.)* Shit. Mona! get me Bill back on the phone.

DOT: It's not science, Dad. It's physics. The physics of falling objects. In this case, you. The physics of my dad the falling object. I'm making a presentation and I need to know some stuff. So it's important that you be as honest and as accurate as possible.

MICHAEL: *(On the phone.)* …Well where is he? We were just…I'll be back up there shortly. It's only temporary! Look…listen…tell him…tell Bill we should proceed full speed ahead. Timing is everything. Yeah, tell Bill that… No. He can't. …Well, I'm not in my office. *(Hangs up.)* Dot! Dot! What floor am I on?

DOT: I don't know. It hasn't quite been a second yet. At one second you will have fallen nine point eight meters. Actually, you're still right up there. Kind of lovely, isn't it? Now then. First question. How high are your ceilings? If your ceilings are eight feet you're –

MICHAEL: Hang on. I have a call. Hello?

DOT: ...If they're 10 feet... Dad, are your ceilings ten or eight feet?

MICHAEL: Bill!... No, that's what I said to Mona... No, we're gonna double-down on that sonofabitch right now. I'm on my way back up. Right now.

DOT: They say that you pass out before you hit. That you can't possibly stay conscious through the incredible force that is exerted on your body. Before you hit you pass out. What's your hypothesis?

MICHAEL: Dot. Nobody is hitting or passing out... *(In frustration he attempts to manoeuvre to try to unfall his way back up.)*

DOT: Dad, no law of physics in the world is going to get you to unfall your way back up. Your best hope is to pass out.

MICHAEL disappears. MING enters with a chair, sits in it directly in front of DOT. DOT gives MING a quick nod. Enthusiastically she raises her hand. DOT sees it. MING takes notes from time to time with a notepad and pencil.

DOT: Yes?

MING: Can you explain force to me?

DOT: I can. F equals M A. Force equals mass times acceleration. The amount of force exerted on a body is equal to that body's mass multiplied by the rate of its acceleration. Amazing, huh? I mean, that's just the way it is. Every time.

MING puts her hand up again.

DOT: Yes?

MING: So this would mean that a...a grown man's head would have more force than a dead canary?

DOT: More force on what?

MING: Pardon?

DOT: They have to exert their force on something.

MING is thinking.

MING: A car? A sidewalk? A person?

DOT: Excellent. In other words, there is no force until…

MING: …until…impact.

DOT: Precisely. We'll be discussing impact a little later.

Once again MING raises her hand.

DOT: Uh…yes?

MING: And why did you choose your father as your subject?

DOT: No reason. It just seemed so obvious. I mean I estimate his mass to be about 212 pounds or 96 kilograms and he's, like, on the 73rd floor so…

MING: So that's good?

DOT gets closer to MING perhaps sitting down beside her.

DOT: It's good if you're doing a physics experiment on falling objects. Like, this isn't personal. Well ok it is. He's my dad. But see, I need him to fall so other things can happen.

MING: Is he, like, your um…

DOT: Variable?

MING: Right.

DOT: Yes. He's my controlled variable. Constant; predictable. Like no matter what I do he's gonna fall at the same rate all the time. No matter what. And no matter what I do he's going to keep doing what he does. He has to. But his falling's going to change everything. A new direction. A new momentum.

MING: Like how?

DOT: I don't know. It has to.

MING: What has to?

DOT: This.

MING: This?

DOT: *This* is torture. *This* is ridiculous. *This* is an abomination. I mean, what are we? What are we doing?

MING: You mean, like the world?

DOT: No, my family. Is this supposed to be a loving like, family? I mean, come on! *(MING shrugs.)* So I wanted to start brand new. With my dad at V O.

MING: V O?

DOT: Initial velocity. Zero.

MING: Oh.

DOT: And then I thought: My mom. Dependent variable. Perfect.

MING: Dependent variable?

DOT: Yeah. 130 pounds or 58 kilograms and like, on the 2nd floor. She's practically going nowhere. We get to see how she reacts.

MING: To your dad?

DOT: To everything. Especially me. No wait. That's a dependent – my dad would be the independent – no wait…

MING: What am I?

DOT: In the experiment?

MING: Yeah.

DOT: You're my friend. *(She is close enough to MING that she plays with MING's hair.)*

MING: Ok.

DOT: And then I had this project and it was the perfect opportunity to, I don't know, blow things up. Set things off. See what would happen.

MING: What would happen if what?

DOT: If things changed. If I changed things. Me, them, everything.

MING: I would get into so much trouble if I blew up my parents. They would ground me and never talk to me again.

DOT: Your parents are so great. They ignore you.

MING: Your parents ignore you.

DOT: It's a different ignore. With your parents I can feel them everywhere. It's like they're always looking at you…with love. Even if they don't pay any attention to you. They just assume you're going to do what they do.

MING: Isn't that bad?

DOT: *(Sigh.)* Do Zebra moms and dads spend a whole lot of time talking to their kids? No. Do their kids do what their Zebra moms and dads do? Yes. That's why you're such a nice kid.

MING: I'm not that nice.

DOT: You are. You're very nice. You're what I wish I had been.

MING: I can be pretty – (mean when I want to be…)

DOT: My God. If I did what my parents do. I'd have been dead or killed at, like, four.

MING: So how do they do it?

DOT: Do what.

MING: Be your parents.

DOT: They do fucked-up shit and then they sit me down and tell me that they did fucked-up shit and that I should never do it.

MING: Really?

DOT: Watch.

LAURA and MICHAEL appear. MICHAEL is not falling. They stand there waiting.

DOT: Go.

LAURA and MICHAEL enter into a full-tilt, post-party fight.

LAURA: That's not what Gord told me!

MICHAEL: Gord? What the hell does Gord know? He's got his head so far up his ass, he chews on his…goddamn tonsils.

LAURA: Well he certainly knows you. He managed to predict your actions to a T.

MICHAEL: Predict my actions? Predict my – ? Who was licking Tucker's ear for Chrissake?

Who spilled her 5th Goddamn martini all over herself and then suggested that Brian lick it up?

LAURA: It was a joke!

MICHAEL: Some joke. Some fucking joke.

LAURA: Did he lick it off me? No! He did not lick it off me. If I had wanted him to lick it off me, by God, he would have!

MICHAEL: My mother said that about you 20 times.

LAURA: What? That I liked to have men lick drinks off me?

MICHAEL: That you liked attention. Male attention.

LAURA: I like any attention. Some attention. It's the only male attention I get!

MICHAEL: That is not fair. Between you and Dot, it's all I ever hear.

LAURA: Well, excuse me! And Dot's your daughter.

MICHAEL: So?

LAURA: Oh, good answer. So? I can understand how that would be meaningless to you.

LAURA and MICHAEL stop abruptly.

DOT: Amazing. Somehow every fight comes back to me.

LAURA: And your mom's a lying hag!

They are gone. MING raises her hand.

DOT: Yes?

MING: …Wow.

LAURA enters but remains at a distance. She has been crying. It's part of the previous fight.

DOT: Hi Mom.

LAURA: I'm going out for a while.

DOT: Kay.

LAURA: There's food in the fridge.

DOT: Kay.

>   *Pause.*

LAURA: That's not how all adults act. Couples.

DOT: Ok.

>   *Pause. LAURA exits.*

DOT: Me and my parents just make for a great experiment, don't you think?

>   *MING raises her hand.*

DOT: Yes?

MING: What are you doing later?

DOT: Nothing, what are you doing?

MING: Do you want to hang out? Can you take me to a party or something?

DOT: Won't your parents be mad?

MING: Not if they don't know.

DOT: Um…I don't think that's such a –

MING: I think Jee's cute.

DOT: Yeah. *(Pause.)* So's Zoo. Zoo's cute. Have you met Zoo?

>   *MICHAEL appears falling, busily trying to make cell phone contact.*

MICHAEL: Dammit! Dot!

DOT: Gotta go. Come back later.

MING: Kay.

MICHAEL: Dot!

DOT: What!

MICHAEL: My speed is screwing up my phone. Bill may be trying to reach me!

DOT: It's not your speed. That's so juvenile. That's when you have no direction. This is your velocity, Dad. Velocity's all about direction. In this case, down.

LAURA appears.

LAURA: All right. Fine. I'm here. Dot, my phone please. *(She looks to MICHAEL, more annoyed than incredulous.)* What are you doing?

DOT: Mom! Finally! You're here! *(DOT snaps a picture of her mom.)*

IMAGE #4: A shot of Laura in a jump suit
in an exercise pose.

MICHAEL: Nothing. Business. I'm trying to do business.

LAURA: I need to talk to you.

LAURA: *(To DOT.)* Well, I can't stay. *(Looking at MICHAEL again.)* What the hell is this?

DOT: It's my project. See, I took Dad and –

LAURA: Dot. I told you. I can't be at your project. *(To DOT.)* Where's my phone?

DOT: Mom, do you think you pass out before you hit?

LAURA: Dot, sweetie, I really need to talk to your father.

DOT: While you're falling. They say you pass out. / That you can't possibly –

MICHAEL: *(Trying to make phone contact.)* Bill?… Bill?

LAURA: I don't have time –

DOT: Mom, just answer –

LAURA: Fine! It's a myth.

DOT: What? Why?

LAURA: No time.

MICHAEL: There. Ya see? There's no time, now if you'll excuse me… *(He resorts to his phone.)*

DOT: Wow, that's true. There's no time. That's a great hypothesis, Mom. Right now, Dad, given the floor you started on and the height of each floor, I estimate it will take you a total of 6 seconds before you hit the ground. That's fast. Faster every second. Like, at second 5 you will be travelling 19.6 meters per second. But not squared. That nine point eight meters per second, per second? Like, squared? That's your acceleration. If only we were just dealing with acceleration here. But we're not. We're talking velocity. There's a huge difference. I mean your acceleration is predictable. Constant. But the bitch is that we have to deal with that motherfucker velocity.

MICHAEL: You are not allowed to say motherfucker.

DOT: You say motherfucker all the time.

MICHAEL: It's a business term. It's just business. How fast by the time I land? Maybe if I hurry this up *(He tries to "hurry it up.")*

DOT: Uh…there'll be no "landing" here, Dad. Sorry. And I haven't calculated the final velocity yet. But it'll be pretty wild. Especially from, like, 73 floors.

LAURA: 74.

DOT: 73, Mom.

LAURA: 74. There's "G". The ground floor.

DOT: But there's no 13th floor. They cancel each other out. 73. Well, he used to be at the 73rd floor.

LAURA: *(To DOT.)* Are you putting on weight?

DOT: No.

LAURA: You look like you're putting on weight.

DOT: I'm not.

LAURA: Is that my makeup you're wearing?

DOT: No.

LAURA: That's not my eye shadow?

DOT: No.

LAURA: It looks like my eye shadow.

DOT: It's not.

LAURA: It's the same colour.

DOT: It's not.

LAURA: Identical.

DOT: It's not your eye shadow. *(To audience.)* It's not her fucking eye-shadow.

LAURA: Michael. I don't have all day. I have places to be.

MICHAEL: Dot, you'll have to cancel your experiment. I'll…I'll write a note to your teacher.

DOT: Everyone falls at the same rate. Isn't that amazing? Everyone. Everything. A fat man. A little baby. A brick, a piece of paper, a penny. Amazing.

LAURA: I would like to speak.

DOT: Once acceleration gets a hold of you velocity just goes all fuckin' nuts.

LAURA: I would like to SPEAK!! *(Silence.)* First of all, Michael, you should know that I do not love you.

DOT: Should I write this down? *(She does.)*

MICHAEL: Not now, Laura! God, it's cold up here!

DOT: *(Writing.)* The subject felt a drop in temp –

LAURA: I have come to realize it over several years. But I can probably say with a great degree of certainty that I never loved you.

DOT: *(Writing.)* …Never…loved…

MICHAEL: That's bullshit! *(Into phone.)* No, not you, Mona.

LAURA: It's true.

DOT: It is. *(To audience.)* My mom doesn't love him. She never has. Ever since I was born, or soon after, I remember the look she gave him when I came out *(Imitates the look.)*.

LAURA: And that brings me to my next little piece of information: I think I'm pregnant.

DOT: What? *(To the audience, really.)* Oh fuck right off, Mom.

LAURA: I…I'm having a baby.

MICHAEL: You just think you are.

DOT: Dad. Any woman who thinks she's pregnant usually is.

LAURA: That's true.

DOT: For example, I don't think I'm pregnant.

MICHAEL: I hope you don't think you're pregnant. Why would you think –

DOT: Oh, I've thought it before. That I've been pregnant. But then I think about it for a while and then think I'm probably not. And then…I'm not. I always wonder if – for that little bit of time that I think I'm pregnant – that maybe I actually am pregnant. And then I just think the whole thing right out of me. And then I get my period and I'm not. It's worked every time. I can't imagine a more powerful or more convenient method of birth control. It's like if cartoon characters could get pregnant. One minute they'd be pregnant and the next they'd be like, not. Abortions would be so easy. It'd be like, the Little Mermaid or something walking along all pregnant in one frame and everybody would be all hey weren't you pregnant? and the Little Mermaid would be like, nuh-uh. Do I look pregnant to you? And everybody would forget all about it.

LAURA: You are not allowed to get pregnant, young lady.

DOT: How come you can get pregnant and I can't?

LAURA: You're 15. And you're my daughter.

DOT: *(To audience.)* The two things she most regrets about me. She has no idea how fertile I am right now. I could smell a fucking tulip or look at a rabbit the wrong way and I'd be… *(She demonstrates pregnancy by extending her belly awkwardly.)*

LAURA: And I'm leaving you.

MICHAEL: What?

DOT: *(Louder.)* She's leaving you!

LAURA: It's not personal... Ok. Sorry. It is. It is personal.

MICHAEL: Personal? Why?

LAURA: I can't tell you. It's personal.

MICHAEL: I am just about to broker something big! I had
Bill on the phone. Bill. Do you know how big Bill is? He's
huge.

DOT: What's his mass? If you tell me his / mass I could –

MICHAEL: He's on the 85th floor. You know where I'm headed
after all this?

DOT: The 85th floor?

MICHAEL: The 85th floor. Or 83 or 4 at least. Do you have any
idea what the view is like from the 85th floor?

DOT: I'm asking the questions around here. I'm doing a
project!

LAURA: Enough with your project and your...your ninety
percent average.

DOT: Ninety-four.

MICHAEL: We were perfect, Laura. Perfect. Your...fitness stuff.
Dot in piano lessons...

DOT: ...I'm quitting.

LAURA: You are not quitting. It's the only worthwhile thing
you do.

MICHAEL: Wait till you hear about this deal Bill's got me
working on, Laura. It's fantastic. Huge. This tumble I'm
taking right now? Temporary. Momentary.

DOT: Dad, does this look temporary to you? Look how
fast that ground is moving up to meet you. It's going to
happen. So you better enjoy doing the deal and being all
snazzy because shit's goin down!

MICHAEL: This deal's going down. That's what's going down!
Now, you stop your project.

DOT: I can't, ok? You are going to go splat. Right there on the pavement. If you're lucky you might bounce off something. An awning, a gargoyle, a postal truck. God, that would be cool. *(DOT steps forward. For the moment she's the only one lit. She shares the dream with the audience. Perhaps the slightest hint of music.)* I saw a picture once. It was beautiful. Black and white from an old *Life Magazine* or something... A woman, a very beautiful woman, blond, Marilyn hair, the darkest lips and the whitest skin, threw herself off of a building. A tall building, like my dad's building, and landed on top of a car. The roof. She was dead. The roof just gave way perfectly to her body like a hammock. She was still so beautiful. No blood, no bruises, just laying there on her side. Her skirt still modestly covering her thighs the way it should. Wouldn't that be great? To die beautiful? I don't need to die peacefully, or painlessly. Some people want to die spectacular. I want to die beautiful. *(A lighting change and MICHAEL re-appears, falling.)*

...Or Asian, Mom! I could die Asian!

LAURA: Well you couldn't. You can't die Asian. To die Asian you'd have to be Asian and you can't be Asian. There are already a zillion of them and you aren't one.

DOT: You're just saying that because I wasn't born Asian.

LAURA: There's a reason you weren't born Asian. *(Points to MICHAEL.)* Does he look Asian to you?

MICHAEL: Or sure, blame me.

DOT: Asians seem to have so much going for them, don't they, Mom? I know there's, like a hundred or something different countries in Asia but I think the idea of being Asian is, in general, very attractive. *(Mysterious with a fake accent.)* Orrriiieeeeeennnntaaaaaallllllll. We're all very beautiful.

MICHAEL: She doesn't even look Asian.

LAURA: Oh my God, that is so racist.

DOT: I wonder. Do I have to look Asian to be Asian?

MICHAEL: How would I know you're Asian if you don't look Asian?

MICHAEL has stopped falling; like a cartoon character who has a sudden thought or epiphany and simply stops for a moment.

LAURA: How do you know someone's Polish? Or German or…or African?

MICHAEL: African? *(Newly freaked.)* Holy shit. That's the street! My God, I can…I can see the street!

LAURA: I can't deal with this now. It's upsetting me and I have an audition. *(She starts to go and then turns back.)* I'll come back when…when you're not…doing whatever it is that you're doing and we can talk about… *(LAURA trails off, glancing at DOT.)*

DOT: Dividing the spoils? Once again it all comes down to me.

LAURA begins to exit. DOT is yelling off but LAURA is gone.

DOT: Who gets *me*!?… Who gets *me*!? *(She looks at the audience. Quietly.)* Who gets me? *(LAURA is gone. DOT looks off for a moment then turns to her falling father.)* Are you ready Dad?

MICHAEL: Ready for what?

DOT: *(Deliberately to the audience.)* …Five!

There is an abrupt lighting change and the sound of something streaking through the air. MICHAEL is suddenly falling again as though he's just been reminded. He makes noise like he's lost breath or is in fear. DOT takes a photo of him. It flashes on screen.

IMAGE 5: A Dot and Michael selfie. On holiday
or hanging at home. It's casual but Michael's
face and mouth and arms make him look like
he's falling.

MING appears again with a chair staring into her phone. She puts the phone away and sits and raises her hand.

MING: What's his current velocity?

DOT: Second 2 brings him to nineteen point six. Meters. Per second. See Dad? Look how much faster you're falling in just one second.

MICHAEL: What? That was one second? That took forever.

DOT: Oh. The early seconds do. But each second speeds up.

MING: How is that possible?

DOT: Oh, it's not. Actually my dad's accelerating. But he's covering more ground – or distance – with each second.

MING: Second Squared?

DOT: No. Listen now. That's his rate of acceleration. Constant. But his velocity is always changing. Always. In the time I just blinked *(She blinks.)* he's got a new velocity.

MING puts her hand up again. She is looking at her phone at the same image of MICHAEL as we have just seen.

DOT: Yes?

MING: Was there ever a time when he was not accelerating?

DOT: No. The nature of his life is that he is very prone to acceleration. He wants his world to go faster and then he's created something he can't stop. He's consumed by it.

MING: And everyone accelerates at the same rate?

DOT: They do when they make someone want to explode them out of an office tower.

MING: Are you suggesting that he brought this upon himself?

DOT: Yes.

MING: How?

DOT: *(Thinks.)* Ok. Watch.

The lights change. Only DOT and MICHAEL are illuminated. MICHAEL is not falling for a moment. He becomes casual, and controlled. Perhaps he's reading something or watching TV. We are in a different time and place.

DOT: Dad?

MICHAEL: Hmm?

DOT: I'm going out with a boy tonight.

MICHAEL: Don't be out too late.

Pause.

DOT: Where's Mom?

MICHAEL: At a meeting.

DOT: She's always at a meeting.

MICHAEL: Not always.

DOT: Always.

MICHAEL: Is there something you wanted to tell her? Because you can tell me.

DOT stands there and looks at MICHAEL whose attention is already elsewhere. She debates whether to say anything. She takes a breath.

DOT: I am going to have sex tonight. It is going to be the first time I ever have sex. It is going to occur on the basement floor in this house of this boy I barely know but just chatted with online. He seems cool. It is going to be without protection. It is going to hurt enough but I'll be quiet because his little brother is playing Grand Theft Kill Destroy Rape Video Game on the other side of the black pleather couch. The actual act is going to take 40 seconds ending in the boy's spunky sperm running down my leg and onto the shag carpet where he's going to make it disappear by smushing his foot into it. This will occur because at the last second I force him to pull out because he never would have himself because either he has no idea what actually is supposed to happen or he assumes that I know what I'm doing and that I understand what measures should be taken to ensure non-pregnancy etcetera. Which I do. Entirely by accident. By hearing other girls speak about it in the same way they talk about blush or shampoo. I am going to be sad and I am going to walk in the house and you are going to be asleep on the couch and Mom is already going to be in bed and I am going to regret that my parents who grill me over everything whether they give a shit or not, weren't here to grill me on what I did that night because at least then I would be forced to lie. To do something other than nothing.

A pause. MICHAEL looks up.

MICHAEL: Is there something you wanted to tell her? Because you can tell me.

DOT: No.

Lights go out on MICHAEL and come back up on MING. She raises her hand.

MING: Did that really happen?

DOT: Doesn't matter. Nothing matters.

DOT lifts up a brown paper bag. It's her dad's lunch.

MING: What's that?

DOT: His lunch.

MING: And you are going to have lunch with your dad?

DOT: Sort of.

MING: Did you make it?

DOT: Oh no. I have no idea how to make a lunch. I've never made a lunch before in my life.

MING: Who did?

Immediately lights come up on ZOO and JEE. They are dancing in that casual, cool sort of way. Something ZOO does suggests a desire – an attempt – to imitate JEE even as lights flash around them. MING exits with her chair.

DOT: *(To the audience.)* Young men are the most dangerous. They will do or say anything to anybody. They believe they will not die and if they do it won't matter because it will be glorious. They will fuck dogs or your grandmother with equal passion. They will kill pigeons or the president of the United States with the same relish and abandon. They have no future beyond that which they can stuff into their mouths, nose, or ass within the next two hours. They have found a spirituality from their boredom and that spirituality is death. Glorious and spectacular. And they can watch themselves, their friends, their heroes find that death or something that looks like it on a million Youtube shows on a million websites, on a million TV channels created just for them. They are Arab, Greek, East African, West African, African American, Anglo-Saxon, Hispanic, Asian, Filipino, East Indian, West Indian, American Indian, Polish, German, Jew, Muslim, Christian, atheist, evangelist, fundamentalist... And if you find them quickly enough, before they become tired, worn, comfortable, fat, bouncing from meeting to meeting in their misguided ties, selling samples strapped into their briefcases...they will wear your bomb around their belly. *(DOT snaps a photo of them.)*

IMAGE #6: Jee and Zoo. They are in a pose
at a party shirts off, sweaty. Jee has a blue pill
on his tongue.

DOT: *(Quietly.)* Go.

JEE: 2:30 in the AM. She walks over to me with this grin like she swallowed the best tasting shit ever. I'm like, "What." She just grabs me by the back of the head and sticks her tongue down my throat. I'm like, "what the fuck was that for?" But not, like, mad or anything, just like, "what'd you do that for?"

ZOO: Yeah.

JEE: Then she looks at Zoo here and she takes him by the back of the head and kisses him. And I'm like, "who the fuck are you?" And she goes, "I'm the best thing that's ever happened to you." So we dance – the three of us – close just like this until four in the morning. Then we take her home and climb into the back of her mom's SUV and drop something onto our tongues that make us all repeat the word "yellow" over and over again.

DOT lets out a squeal and runs over to join them dancing.

ZOO: She's a goddess. A post-modern goddess.

DOT: That's post-post-modern goddess.

JEE: Are you hot for her Zoo?

ZOO: No. Yeah. Uh…

JEE: You are. I can tell you are.

ZOO: I'm not, ok?

JEE: You're not hot for me are you?

ZOO: No.

JEE: Then don't dance so fuckin close.

ZOO: Sorry.

MICHAEL appears falling and notices them.

MICHAEL: Stay away from my daughter!

JEE: Dude, she's fuckin hardcore.

ZOO: Hardcore, dude.

MICHAEL: Stay away from her! She's 15!

JEE: We can't! She's such a fuckin little gangbanger.

ZOO: She is! She's a gangbanger!

DOT: Look at me, Dad. I'm a gangbanger!

MICHAEL: You are not allowed to be a gangbanger!

DOT steps right back in to dance with the boys again.

JEE: You're quite the gangbanger yourself, Mr. D.

MICHAEL: I am not a gangbanger. I just got off the phone with the president of…the…he's on the 85th floor!

ZOO: 85th floor? I'd call that some serious gangbangin.

JEE: But it looks like you're getting gangbanged now, Mr. D.

ZOO: It is. I guess it was time you got gangbanged back.

Snap change. ZOO and JEE are gone. MICHAEL disappears. MING re-enters with her chair, places it down, raises her hand.

MING: I'm beginning to understand. So your dad is getting gangbanged?

DOT: He is now.

MING: Is your mom getting gangbanged too?

DOT: No. Well, maybe. I think she may be gangbanging herself.

MING: Are Zoo and Jee gangbangers?

DOT: They're big gangbangers. I mean, sometimes I have no idea what they're going to do but that just makes it way more fun. They're, like, my major independent variables. They're, like, variables of variables.

MING: Are they going to gangbang your mom?

DOT: Let's watch and see. Shall we?

MING: Kay.

LAURA appears. DOT takes the hands of both boys and marches them over to LAURA. MING moves her chair to a better viewpoint. The boys are not dancing now. A different time and place.

DOT: Mom, these are my friends, Zoo and Jee.

LAURA looks at them both. JEE is looking at his phone.

LAURA: Nice to meet you.

ZOO: Hey.

JEE: Whutsup, Mrs. D?

LAURA: You can call me Laura.

JEE: Whutsup, Laura.

LAURA: So, how do you know these boys?

DOT: I met them at a party.

LAURA: A party. What kind of party?

DOT: *(Sarcastic.)* A heroin-crack-orgy party. What do you mean what kind of party?

LAURA: I don't know. Like, a "rave" party or something?

DOT: Yeah. Sure. A "rave" party.

LAURA: And what do you boys do?

ZOO: Party.

LAURA: That's it? You party?

JEE: Zoo's a freak.

ZOO: I'm not a –

JEE: We go to school.

LAURA: You both go to school.

ZOO: Yeah. Sometimes.

LAURA: And Jee?

JEE: Uh-huh?

LAURA: And where do you come from, Jee?

JEE: Here.

LAURA: No. Like, originally.

JEE: Here.

LAURA: No. I mean your parents.

A pause. JEE has no idea what she even means.

DOT: Jee's in college.

LAURA: College.

ZOO: I'm in high school.

DOT: When he feels like it.

ZOO: Yeah. Sometimes. When I feel like it.

LAURA: And Jee, what are you studying?

JEE: *(Shrugs.)* I don't know. Business.

LAURA: Business.

JEE: Yeah. Business admin, like.

ZOO: I like math and social studies.

LAURA: *(To JEE.)* Don't you think you're a little old for my daughter? I mean look at her. She's still a child. She barely has boobs yet.

DOT: Mom!

ZOO: 15's perfect.

JEE: Yeah. It's all downhill after that. *(They look at DOT.)* Don't think we'll be, like, hanging out with your daughter at, like, 16.

ZOO: Yeah. Gross. Just kidding, Dot.

JEE: But she's fuckin hot right now.

ZOO: Totally hot.

JEE: *(To DOT.)* I gotta go. Text me.

DOT: Ok.

JEE races off. ZOO remains there for a moment. They have distanced themselves from LAURA.

ZOO: Dot.

DOT: Yeah?

ZOO: So I have this idea for your experiment.

DOT: Uh-huh?

ZOO: So I was thinking we could go out sometime and do something.

DOT: Zoo, we do stuff all the time.

ZOO: Yeah, but, like. Just with me, maybe.

An uneasy overlap…

DOT:
Oh. Well. That's be…um…

ZOO:
Yeah…yeah. And I could tell you what I'm thinking about, you know, about your, like –

DOT:
It'd be fine if you wanted to like, talk about Like, um…you know…how…

ZOO:
I don't know – we could, like…

DOT:
But Jee's kind of, you know…

ZOO:
So, yeah. Yeah. I wasn't sure. I can just, like or whatever. *(To LAURA.)* Your daughter's fuckin hot…

Laura. She's really cool too.

LAURA:

That's…nice, Zoo.

ZOO:

Yeah. *(Pause.)* Yeah.

They all just stand for a moment in silence.

DOT: You ok, Zoo?

ZOO: Yeah. Oh yeah. *(Pause. ZOO exits. MING raises her hand.)*

MING: Is Zoo ok?

DOT: Yeah. He's just…he's 17.

MING: Yeah. *(She raises her hand again.)*

DOT: Just wait. It's not finished. *(DOT re-directs her attention to her mom.)*

LAURA: That Jee seems to be an interesting guy.

DOT: Yeah. They're both pretty cool.

LAURA: Is that my outfit?

DOT: No.

LAURA: That's not my top?

DOT: It's not your outfit. I wouldn't fit into your outfit.

Pause.

LAURA: Are you seeing one of them?

DOT: Not really.

LAURA: Have you slept with either of them?

DOT: Why do you want to know?

LAURA: I have a right.

DOT: Would you like it if I was?

LAURA: That's up to you. You're a big girl.

DOT: I'm 15.

LAURA: Well, you are on the pill.

DOT: I know. Why is that, Mom?

LAURA: It was a suggestion.

DOT: You're paying for them.

LAURA: Well…I didn't put you on the pill because I thought all you were going to do was grope and grind.

DOT: Ok. We grope and grind.

LAURA: You don't have sex? You're…you're not having sex?

DOT: With who?

LAURA: I don't know who. One of them.

DOT: Which one of them?

LAURA: Which one of them do you want to have sex with?

DOT: Which one of them do you want me to have sex with?

LAURA: I don't care which one you have sex with. Have sex with them all. Go ahead!

DOT: I think you do care.

LAURA: Why? Why should I care!?

DOT: I don't know…Mom.

   Pause.

LAURA: Is Jee Muslim?

DOT: No. I don't know. Why? Does it make you afraid? Does it turn you on?

LAURA: He looks Muslim.

DOT: How does he look Muslim?

LAURA: He just / does, that's all.

DOT: And what difference does that make?

LAURA: Never mind.

   A pause. LAURA says to herself, "where's my phone?". She exits.

MING: Did your mom just gangbang you?

DOT: It sorta felt like it.

MING: Why?

DOT: My hypothesis? It's cause she truly loves me but her world is so crowded with – excuse the language – shit, that she can't, in a way, see me.

MING: So she's…

DOT: Kind of a hag right now.

MING: No, like in science.

DOT: Oh. Dependent variable. One of them. We have to watch when shit happens to her.

MING: How?

In the background, LAURA has been fading into the scene. She's rolled in her chair and is primping and adjusting herself as she prepares for the audition. ZOO now appears beside her in another swivel chair. He is vaguely dressed as a morning talk show host. Somehow, though, it is obvious it is ZOO (to us – not to LAURA). There is only a small attempt to look like another character. LAURA appears slightly nervous but competent. Perhaps she is trying just a bit too hard to be cool, hip, youngish. The two banter stylishly. Please note the / to indicate overlap. Actors should feel free to play regardless of the stage directions.

A slight pause, then they're "on".

LAURA: Good morning.

ZOO: Good morning.

LAURA: Morning, Gary.

ZOO: Morning to you, Laura. You look fantastic, by the by. Is that…? What is that?

LAURA: What's what?

ZOO: That blouse. / What is that?

LAURA: Rayon… Yeah…rayon…I think it's rayon. *(Looking off.)* I'm…Margaret is…is this rayon? / It is. It is rayon. Isn't it.

ZOO: Rayon. Wow. How come I don't get rayon stuff?

LAURA: Apparently it's rayon. It just shapes my body so –

ZOO: Who knew rayon / could be such a...such a cool, flowy kind of...

LAURA: It suits certain body types really really well. It really / does.

ZOO: So! What are we talking about this morning? Who's on first?

LAURA: What's on second?

ZOO: What? *(Pause. They laugh. They stop.)* You look hot, Laura.

LAURA: *(Slight pause.)* We have a...fantastic day ahead of us here on City Morning, and I'm so glad you're with us. I really am. Gary, what...what are you doing?

ZOO: I'm trying...I'm trying to check the label to see what kind of material this is. Maybe I have rayon too.

LAURA: Time to move on, Gary. Time to move on I think / if we could just –

ZOO: All right. All right. / I'm movin on.

LAURA: We're moving on. It's a beautiful day out there today with nary a chance a rain...

ZOO: Ha. Nary.

LAURA: What? Pardon?

ZOO: Nary? Who says nary? What does nary even mean?

LAURA: "Not", Gary. It means not, / you know like...

ZOO: Nary, nary quite contrary.

LAURA: "Not", Gary that's what it means. Not a chance. As in there's no chance of rain. None.

Pulsating techno music is heard. The lights start to flash on them as they sit in their swivel chairs. "Gary" starts to gyrate even as he continues to sit in his chair.

ZOO: Ok. Ok. Sorry, just trying to liven things up a bit, you know.

LAURA: Speaking of live, we'll have a guest coming up in a few minutes –

ZOO: Did you get a lip job for this audition, Laura?

LAURA: What? No, I –

ZOO: I did. Not for this but for…like, in general. What do you think of them, Laura?

LAURA: Uh…they're really…

ZOO: How 'bout a kiss, Laura?

LAURA: I don't think our viewers really –

ZOO: Wow. You need a fuckin sense of humour. Seriously. Can we get a co-host who has a sense of humour?

LAURA: I don't…I'm…I'm not…

ZOO: Are you like this with your daughter? Is this how you communicate with Dot?

LAURA: …We have several really hot guests with us this morning…

ZOO: This whole thing is lame. Ridiculously lame. Stupid.

Awkwardness. LAURA stares blankly out into the space in front of her. ZOO/GARY is simply gyrating in his chair with a goofy smile on his face. Lights out on the swivel chairs. DOT steps into their light and in front of them. She is laughing hysterically.

DOT: Oh my God, that was awesome! *(She collects herself.)* Four!

Lighting change. The sound of an object swooshing through the air. Lights up on MICHAEL. He is on the phone, falling. DOT snaps a picture.

IMAGE #7: Michael falling – a different
position and a slightly different backdrop look
behind him. He appears more frantic than ever.

At the same time ZOO and JEE appear with their dancing, lighting and techno music. They are both looking at phones at the same time, seeing that image.

ZOO: *(To MICHAEL.)* Holy shit. How long's he been falling?

DOT: It seems long and short at the same time. But really? Going on 3 seconds.

MICHAEL: No! Bill! I said "calling" – not "falling".

JEE: Wow. 3 seconds? That takes him to what? The 50th floor?

ZOO: I think more like the 40th.

MICHAEL: *(On phone.)* No. I'm still...yes sir, still totally on board!

JEE: The 40th?

ZOO: Yeah.

JEE: How could it be the 40th?

ZOO: He's accelerating. He's not going past the floors at the same rate all the way down...

MICHAEL: Dot! Do you see what's happening here?

DOT: I do! You're already exceeding, like 30 something meters per second. That's a killer velocity. I mean you could kill someone going that speed.

ZOO: ...See, Jee, if it took him point four two seconds to go, say, 3 floors between second 6 and second 5, it'll take him, I don't know, probably less than point two seconds to cover the same number of floors between second 4 and second 3.

MICHAEL: If this deal gets screwed, Dot, someone's going to be in a lot of trouble.

DOT: You mean you?

MICHAEL: This is not fucking up. Do you hear me?

DOT: That's the challenge, Dad. You're my control variable. You're not allowed to fuck up.

MICHAEL: Damn. My ear's starting to bleed!

DOT: Cool!

JEE: Hey, Zoo's right, man. This is not your easy-going velocity equals distance over time.

ZOO: Yeah. That's just that pussy v equals d over t shit. This is final.

JEE: It's the great hand of gravity, man. Eventually it reaches out to everything… *(He reaches skyward with one hand while simultaneously getting down on one knee.)* …and slam!

He slams his hand down on the floor. JEE, ZOO, and MICHAEL are gone. Immediately lights come up on MING as she pushes the bed back on the stage and hops on it. A different time and place. She's reading a "Cosmo" magazine (or something adult-like) and has the purse that DOT offered to give her earlier. It's quite snazzy.

MING: Dot. What does "giving head" mean?

The lights come up on ZOO, JEE and DOT as they lay or sit on the floor staring up. ZOO lays in the middle. MING remains lit for the moment. MING is not in the same "scene" as the others.

DOT: Ming asked me what giving head was.

JEE: What'd you tell her?

ZOO: Who's Ming?

MING: *(From the bed.)* Why is everybody always talking about giving head?

JEE: She actually asked you that?

ZOO: I talk about getting head.

DOT: She's never done it.

ZOO: Hard to do it if you don't know what it is.

JEE: Dot's a pro.

ZOO: Yeah.

DOT: Thanks. *(The light on MING goes out.)*

JEE: Whoa. And in your mom's SUV.

ZOO: Yeah. I thought about your mom.

DOT: My mom?

ZOO: She's hot, Dot.

JEE: She is pretty hot.

ZOO: I'd totally do her.

DOT: Gross. Jee?

JEE: Yeah?

DOT: Would you?

JEE: Probably. *(Thinks.)* Oh fuck. Yeah. Totally.

DOT: Would you do my dad?

Pause.

ZOO: I'd do your dad.

DOT: You know, I'd like to do my dad, too.

ZOO/JEE: What?

JEE: Gross.

DOT: Not like that.

JEE: Like what?

> IMAGE #8: A series of montage images all of Michael falling. They are like a smooth slide show of Michael seen to be "wheeling and dealing" on the phone, laughing, holding papers, etc. He looks confident, in control.

DOT, ZOO, and JEE all look at the images projected.

ZOO: Wow.

JEE: He's good.

DOT: I just think his world needs to be fucked around with.

ZOO: Totally.

They watch him.

DOT: Oh my God.

JEE: What.

The images fade out.

DOT: My science project!

JEE: Your science proj –

DOT: Physics! Oh my God. It would be so cool! My dad!

JEE: I don't think it would work.

ZOO: It could. Depends.

JEE: He looks so together…

DOT: I know. It's all about that.

JEE: What.

DOT: Looks. He and mom spend all their time looking like they're this and that. Like they're sexy, rich, horny, sincere, like they love me. *(MICHAEL disappears.)*

JEE: Your parents don't love you? They sure look like they love you.

DOT: See?

JEE: Dude, your dad lets you do whatever you want.

DOT: I know. I mean he'd kill me if he knew I was giving head. But he's the kind of guy who's gotten head since he was 14. Hey, maybe one of those girls was me.

JEE: Cool. I get it. *(Pause.)* But you don't give a shit about your dad.

DOT: This is not about my dad.

JEE: What's it about?

DOT: I don't know. Something else.

ZOO: It's about fucking up the world.

DOT: Not the world my world.

ZOO: What? Why would you –

JEE: How are you going to do it?

DOT: Do what?

JEE: Your dad.

DOT: I don't know. *(Pause.)* Zoo? *(DOT snuggles up to ZOO. Maybe touches him teasingly.)*

ZOO: *(Off in a dream world.)* Yeah?

DOT: What are you thinking?

ZOO: *(Pause.)* Nothing.

DOT: Could you help us…me? *(She gets closer. He looks at her, gets hard.)*

ZOO: Maybe. What floor does he work on?

Lights out on ZOO and JEE. They exit. Lights up on MING in the bed looking at the magazine. DOT joins her on it.

DOT: It's not that gross.

MING: Why would anyone want to do that? Give head.

DOT: It's not about want.

MING: What's it about?

DOT: *(Thinks.)* You're there, ok? And, like, they're, like, with you. Hanging out.

MING: They?

DOT: Ok. Him. Whatever. And you're just talking and after a while it just seems like a good idea. They just seem so into it and everything.

MING: I don't think I could ever do that.

DOT: It's ok.

MING: I don't even have a boyfriend.

DOT: Neither do I.

MICHAEL appears at the bed. It's as though he's in the scene in DOT's room.

MICHAEL: Dot…

MING: I love your room. I love the pink.

DOT: Thanks. I'm anxious for you to meet my mom. She designed it.

MICHAEL: Dot.

DOT: Hi daddy. This is Ming.

MICHAEL: Hello, Ming. Dot I'm going out.

MING: Hello.

DOT: Ming goes to my school.

MICHAEL: That's nice. I'm going out.

DOT: Did you and mom have another fight?

MICHAEL: I need to cool off for a while.

DOT: At a strip club?

MICHAEL: I do not – I am not going to a strip club.

DOT: Dad.

MICHAEL: Yes, Dot.

DOT: Did you get head when you were a boy?

MICHAEL: I beg your pardon?

DOT: Do they give head at strip clubs?

MICHAEL: *(Changing subjects.)* Your mother's downstairs.

DOT: Crying her eyes out and smoking?

MICHAEL: Your mother doesn't smoke. You should go talk to her.

DOT: Isn't that your job? *(Beat.)* Are you guys getting a divorce?

MICHAEL: Of course we're not getting a divorce.

DOT: Cause you can. I won't mind. Maybe we'd get along better and you wouldn't fight over me so much.

MICHAEL: We would never do that to you.

DOT: You already are.

MICHAEL: I have to go.

DOT: To the strip club. Dad, what do you know about physics?

MICHAEL: What?

DOT: I want to do my science project on physics. I like what physics does.

MICHAEL: I don't know anything about physics, Dot.

DOT: You should. I'm doing a project on it. Do you want to be in it?

MICHAEL: Maybe your friend knows something about physics. Lee?

MING: Ming.

MICHAEL: Right. Ming.

DOT: I think Mom's coming up.

MICHAEL: Right.

MICHAEL disappears. LAURA enters DOT's room.

DOT: Hi Mom.

LAURA: Did your father leave?

DOT: Yeah.

LAURA stands there. She's been crying.

DOT: It's ok, Mom. It's not personal. Dad just happens to want something else.

LAURA: He's a bastard. *(Sniff.)*

DOT: He is. Mom, this is Ming.

LAURA: Hello, Ming.

MING: Hello.

DOT: I've been telling Ming about this science project I'm going to do.

LAURA: Science?

DOT: Physics. Falling objects. What would you say if I made Dad my falling object?

LAURA: You mean, splat? Falling? Splat?

DOT: His whole body just spread out on the street like jam on toast.

LAURA: I'd like that.

DOT: Would you? That would show him.

LAURA: That would teach him to ignore me and run off to strip clubs.

MING: Bastard.

DOT: And don't take those strip clubs personally, Mom. I mean those are fucking 18 year olds. Really. Your body's just as nice.

LAURA: Please don't say fuck, Dot.

DOT: And maybe we'd become like a normal family. He'd like you more and you'd appreciate me more and we could eat dinner and have normal –

LAURA: I appreciate you, Dot.

DOT: Not really, Mom. But it would be like you always talk about.

LAURA: What.

DOT: Spending more time with me.

LAURA: Right. *(Pause.)* You don't think I'm drooping a little bit?

DOT: Drooping?

LAURA: Sagging. You know. Down?

DOT: Oh. No way Mom. Right Ming?

MING: Yeah. No way.

LAURA: I mean around the hips. Or jowly maybe? Maybe a new wardrobe?

DOT: We should…if you want we could go shopping for you sometime. You know just, like the two of us. I could show you off at the malls, right? I mean look at you.

LAURA: I try to take care of myself, you know. I do. I just think lately…I don't know…

DOT: Seriously. I could show you some great stores. And we could have lunch and then go to, I don't know, a show later on…

LAURA: *(To MING.)* I have an audition soon.

DOT: I know some incredible stores. I was showing Ming some stuff in one of my magazines? Oh Mom, we could go shopping…I could take you to…and you would totally fit into those outfits. You would. You could, like, wear them at your audition. Oh. And then we could maybe go to the spa and get ourselves all done up... Remember? When we went to that spa that time? Well, like, you and me and those ladies from work. That was so fun. That was, like, like, what was I? Like, 11 or something?

DOT's speech has begun to trail off. She is looking at her mom who has begun to stare at MING.

DOT: ...Mom?

LAURA: Why are Asian girls so perfect?

MING: Pardon?

LAURA: Look at you. You're perfect. Your skin, your hair. Your eyes. How is that possible?

MING: I'm not –

LAURA: Look at this, Dot. Look at her. She just comes like that. A perfect doll. Batteries included. It takes us an hour just to be able to walk out of the house in the morning.

DOT: It doesn't take me an hour –

LAURA has reached out and touched MING's face or hair almost exactly the way DOT did. DOT watches.

LAURA: Why weren't we made like that? Dot? Look at us. Why aren't we fragile? Breakable. Why aren't we like a little piece of precious china?

DOT: I'm breakable.

LAURA: Do you speak Chinese, Ming?

MING: I'm not Chinese.

LAURA: No. Of course. Do they speak Chinese where you're from?

MING: I'm from here.

LAURA: God, you're so cute when you talk.

DOT: Ming has to go. Home. She has to go home. It's late.

LAURA: Maybe she could stay for dinner.

DOT: No.

LAURA: A sleepover. Wouldn't you both –

DOT: Don't you have an audition you have to audition for?

LAURA: *(To MING.)* They're grooming me to be a host on City Morning.

MING: City Morning. Wow. My grandmother watches that every day.

DOT: Go, Mom.

LAURA: Nice meeting you.

MING: You too.

DOT: Bye, Mom.

LAURA exits. A pause.

MING: Your mom's pretty funny.

DOT: Yeah, she's funny. *(Beat.)* She's fucked-up.

MING: Yeah.

DOT gets up and out of bed and takes a long look at MING. MING remains on the bed.

DOT: *(Abruptly.)* You should probably go.

Immediately DOT reaches into her purse/bag and extracts a short, straight-haired wig – a different colour from her own hair – like porn stars or strippers might wear. She also begins to remove some clothing – just enough to turn her into something else – something different, sexual. She does this while she is talking to MING.

MING: Really?

DOT: Yeah. I'm pretty busy right now.

MING: I thought we were going to have –

DOT: *(Takes out her cell phone.)* I'll call your mom to come pick you up. *(DOT puts her phone to her ear and watches MING get out of bed.)*

MING: *(Pause, confused.)* Ok.

DOT: Here. Don't forget this. *(She hands MING the purse. MING, puzzled, rolls the bed off and disappears.)*

DOT: Three!

Immediately sexy lounge-type music plays. DOT begins to dance – as best she can – like a stripper. She looks older, sexier. Her father rolls in front of her in a chair. She's now dancing in front of him. They are in a strip bar.

DOT: You like this?

MICHAEL does not respond. He only sees a hot young stripper. He is on his phone as he watches her.

DOT: Your wife ever dance for you like this?

MICHAEL smiles and shakes his head.

DOT: Who's on the phone?

MICHAEL: Bill. My boss. We're putting together this major acquisition.

DOT: That sounds hot.

MICHAEL: It's a huge deal. He should be here. He'd like you.

DOT: It going to make you rich?

MICHAEL: Richer than I am now.

DOT: That make you hard? Does money make you hard?

MICHAEL: Yeah.

DOT: Am I money? Do you love me like money?

MICHAEL: Yeah. *(MICHAEL forgets about the phone.)*

DOT: Am I making you hard like money?

MICHAEL: Yeah.

DOT: Say it.

MICHAEL: You make me hard. Like money.

DOT: That's a little creepy, Dad. *(She continues to dance. MICHAEL hesitates, looks at her, even while she's still dancing.)*

MICHAEL: What?

MICHAEL stares at her a moment while she continues dancing. She takes off her wig but still dances. Then he "sees" her and he bolts up and begins to back away in this chair while she follows him. It's almost as though he heads back to his "falling position" to escape DOT; or as though DOT chases him back. They speak while he moves away from her.

MICHAEL: What the hell are you doing?

DOT: You like me dancing as a stripper?

MICHAEL: You are not allowed to dance like a stripper!

By now he's falling again, frantically dialing his phone.

DOT: But you loved her. She made you hard!

MICHAEL: Get away from me!

DOT: Just think, Dad. In a couple of years that could be me!

MICHAEL: God, I feel nauseous. *(By now he's falling again.)*

DOT: Oh, right. *(DOT goes and picks up her notebook.)* Nauseous. Good, good! That's excellent. Better watch it or Bill's gonna have you fired.

MICHAEL: He is not. I'm Bill's man. I'm gonna nail that deal. You hear me? See? I'm…I'm on the phone. *(He looks awkward and useless.)* I'm wheeling and I'm deal – *(His phone ringing cuts him off.)* Hello?

JEE appears. He is BILL. He is dressed in a business suit and tie. It is not completely convincing, but initially he seems like a big-time CEO. He holds a phone to his ear. Or has an ear-clip phone. MICHAEL answers his phone. At first he is not looking at MICHAEL falling. DOT listens in, continuing to calculate and interject occasionally.

MICHAEL: Hello?

JEE: Mike. Bill. Where are ya?

MICHAEL: I'm down here on the…50th –

DOT: 43rd.

MICHAEL: – Forty-third floor, Bill.

JEE: What the hell are you doing on 43?

DOT: Forty-two.

JEE: You got some piece of ass you like on 43?

MICHAEL: Yes, sir.

JEE: I need ya up here on 85.

MICHAEL: 85?

JEE: You're familiar with the 85th floor, Mikey?

MICHAEL: Yes, sir.

JEE: Well, I need ya. You're not gonna get squat done on the forty-third floor.

DOT: Forty.

MICHAEL: I know. I'm just not sure –

JEE: We need to dot the I's on this motherfucker.

MICHAEL: Dot the I's.

JEE: Cross the T's, dot the I's, put this bad-boy to bed. You in or not?

MICHAEL: Yes! Yes! I am Bill. I'm just feeling a little…I'm just having a…

JEE: Where are you? What's that sound?

MICHAEL: I'm on the thirty-fifth floor.

DOT: Thirty-four.

JEE: Mickey boy. You can't be dickin around down on the thirty-fifth floor. There's just… What's that sound?

MICHAEL: Sound? I don't hear any –

BILL turns around and sees MICHAEL falling.

JEE: Holy fuck!

DOT: I know, right?

JEE: Mike. What the fuck are you doing?

MICHAEL: It's not what it looks like. Really!

JEE: It looks like you're falling from the motherfucking office tower.

DOT: He is.

JEE: Who's this?

MICHAEL: This my daughter, Dot.

JEE: You never told me you had a daughter.

MICHAEL: I think I did.

JEE: You never told me you had such a good lookin daughter.

MICHAEL: She's 15, Bill.

JEE: Fifteen's such a great age.

MICHAEL: It's a difficult age. Now then. The deal we've –

JEE: Cause the shit sure starts piling up after that. What's she doin over there?

DOT: I'm doing a science project.

JEE: God, I remember when I was 15. I got so much head.

DOT: I probably gave you some of that head.

MICHAEL: Dot!

JEE: So how fast's he falling?

DOT: Well. Do you want his acceleration? His current velocity? His velocity at a particular floor? His terminal velocity…

JEE: You got quite the kid there.

DOT: The explosion just spit him right into the air.

JEE: Who were those two young men leaving your office?

DOT: Zoo and Jee.

JEE: Friends of yours?

DOT: Yeah.

JEE: Good lookin guys that Zoo and Jee. I'll bet you like having fun with them.

DOT: They're fun.

JEE: I bet they are. You party with them?

DOT: Yeah, we party.

JEE: I'll bet you do. They like to dance?

DOT: Yeah.

BILL has begun to remove his jacket, glasses, tie. The thump of techno music is heard. Perhaps the lights around BILL flash slightly.

MICHAEL: Bill, what are you doing?

JEE: Don't you like to party, Mike?

MICHAEL: Bill, I thought we're –

JEE: All work no play, you know what they say, Mikey.

Starts dancing over towards DOT, who stops her calculating and comes over to meet him. They begin to dance. The music becomes louder. They all talk over the music.

MICHAEL: Dot. Dot. You get away from him, you get back to that science project!

DOT: It's physics, Dad. Physics. And since when did you give a crap about my project?

It's clear now that BILL is JEE. He has removed his suit jacket – or whatever else made him "BILL". He and DOT continue to dance.

MICHAEL: You're the reason I'm falling, Dot!

DOT: Physics is the reason you're falling, Dad! Gravity! And I didn't invent gravity. Sir Isaac Newton did.

JEE: Yeah, Mr. D., blame that asshole Newton.

MICHAEL: Where's Bill? What happened to Bill?

DOT: You didn't tell me you had such a hot boss, Dad.

MICHAEL: That's not my boss.

DOT: And East Indian. East Indian guys are very hot.

JEE: I'm West Indian.

DOT: What's a West Indian?

JEE: Just kidding. When white people don't know what you are they call you "Indian".

This LAURA/ZOO scene is a continuation of their last "audition" scene together. Things already seem to be slightly out of control as LAURA seems to be fighting to stay in control. ZOO/GARY is speaking to someone off camera – a completely improvised conversation – about anything. LAURA is still struggling to keep things on track. There is even more overlap.

LAURA: …And we'll have smog and traffic / coming up just 10 minutes past the hour.

ZOO: Looks like we've already got lots of smog and traffic.

LAURA: I meant…I meant the reports. I meant the reports / of smog and traffic.

ZOO: You gotta say what you mean Laura. / Hey I really liked those "Laura's Lessons".

LAURA: Oh, Thank you.

ZOO: I liked that one where you showed off your boobs.

Pause.

LAURA: *(Once again ZOO is speaking to someone off camera all through this.)* Ok… At twenty past the hour this month's fashion feature will…feature a tiny tot fashion show with no fewer than four of metro's up and coming fashion designers. Just a little scaled down, if you know what I mean.

ZOO: I know exactly what you mean. You mean they're little.

LAURA: That's / right, Gary.

ZOO: High fashion for little people.

LAURA: Well, no. Children, / Gary.

ZOO: You have any children, Laura?

LAURA: I do. I have a daughter. She's 15.

ZOO: Wow. 15. That's hot.

LAURA: Actually it's…uh…it's an awkward / age…I think –

ZOO: Hot, hot, hot…hottee.

LAURA: I'm sorry. / I lost my – *(LAURA is frantically searching for the prompt.)*

ZOO: Do you love her, Laura? I mean do you actually love her?

LAURA: I really don't see what –

ZOO: No. No. I'm sure you don't.

LAURA: What's that supposed to mean?

ZOO turns to the audience or TV.

ZOO: In today's three minute segment of "On the Couch" our resident television doctor, Dr. Sanjee talks to Dot about this issue in what we're calling, "Mom, why don't you love me?"

LAURA: This is not – / What the hell is going on?

A lighting change. DOT is sitting up in her bed and DR. SANJEE – who is JEE, poorly disguised again – is sitting on a chair by the bed with a notebook. DOT is crying quietly. DR. SANJEE has a shit-hot East Indian accent.

DOT: And then she said she thought she was pregnant.

JEE: No.

DOT: Yes. And I doubt it's with my dad.

A moment. MING enters with a chair, places it down, sits in it, then lets out a studio audience gasp.

JEE: Get out of town. With who then?

DOT: She won't say. *(JEE is taking notes.)* I think she wants to love me. I really do.

JEE: Do you?

DOT: Yes. Doesn't it make sense? That she'd want to?

JEE: It makes perfect sense. And you. Do you love your mother?

DOT: Oh yes. Very much. *(Deliberately she looks over at her mom.)*

JEE: But you are so mean to her. You make all kinds of disparaging comments.

DOT: It's tough love. She needs help.

LAURA: *(Looking over.)* Dot, what are you doing?

JEE: And how do you propose to help her?

DOT: Well, for one thing I exploded my dad out of his office tower.

JEE: Oh, delightful! Go on.

DOT: It's an attempt to rescue my family.

JEE: It sounds destructive.

LAURA: *(Yelling over.)* I don't need your rescuing. I'm perfectly fine. Look at me. I'm hosting City Morning.

ZOO: *(As the host.)* It's just an audition.

DOT: Mom! I'm right here! This can't be what you want!

ZOO: Whoa this is totally hot. We got, like, MILF-daughter action. *(The faint thump of techno music is heard.)*

DOT: *(Melodramatically, loudly.)* I…just want what's best for my *(Sniff.)* mom, you know?

JEE: Of course I do. *(He takes off his doctor coat and climbs into bed and starts trying to make out with DOT.)*

DOT: No, Jee… No, Doctor Sanjee.

ZOO: Wow. That's hot *(ZOO starts to take his jacket off.)*

LAURA: …Sunny but cool all day today… *(With the techno music playing, ZOO is dancing around while LAURA is trying to talk.)* …The ladies auxiliary of St. Brigid's are going to be "kickin it" tonight as they hold their annual…

ZOO: Come on Laura, you want some of that action?

LAURA: …uh bachelors auction benefit, fundraiser for a cure for…for… *(LAURA finally stomps over to where DOT is fighting off JEE.)* I hope you're happy. I really hope you're –

MING is applauding. Frustrated, LAURA leaves. ZOO comes over. DOT has managed to get off the bed. JEE is attempting to dance with her.

DOT: Not now, Jee. That wasn't supposed to – Mom? …Mom? *(ZOO joins in the dance. It resembles the one earlier.)* …Zoo. No guys, there's no time. Jee…

JEE: All right all right. Later. *(JEE exits, ZOO stops dancing and goes to DOT.)*

ZOO: I need to talk to you.

DOT: Um…ok. Can it wait? I've got a physics experiment to run.

ZOO: That's what I want to – (talk to you about.)

MING is close by.

DOT: Zoo, this is Ming.

ZOO: Hey Ming.

MING: Hi Zoo.

DOT: Ming thinks you're hot.

MING: I do not! Well, I do but…

DOT: She's not really allowed to party. *(Pause. MING tentatively begins to dance with ZOO.)* But she really wants to.

ZOO: Yeah but Dot, I was…

DOT: *(Pause.)* Please Zoo? For me? You'd be doing me a big favour. Can you party with her? She needs to learn how to party. Right Ming? You so want to party, don't you? *(MING shrugs.)* See?

ZOO: Dot –

DOT: Later, Zoo. My dad's probably freaking out by now.

DOT steps away. ZOO yells after her.

ZOO: Dot –

DOT: Two!

Lighting change. Woosh! MING and ZOO are gone. MICHAEL appears falling. He's trying to get service on his phone. He shakes it, hits it, holds in different positons in the air…

DOT: Give it up dad. It's inevitable.

MICHAEL: No. What's inevitable is nailing the account and getting moved up to the 85th floor. That's what's inevitable.

DOT: Your fate was sealed the moment I decided to have lunch with you. Didn't you see those boys who came to your office?

MICHAEL: Boys?

DOT: *(To audience.)* Introducing my dad's lunch!

> *Techno music starts. A scene shift. For a moment MICHAEL does not appear to be falling. ZOO and JEE begin dancing to music under their light. ZOO holds the "lunch" in a brown paper bag. MICHAEL is on the phone, not falling. DOT watches for a moment and then disappears.*

ZOO: Brought you your lunch, Mr. D.

JEE: Brought you your lunch.

MICHAEL: What?

JEE: Your lunch.

ZOO: Smells good.

MICHAEL: What's in it?

JEE: Your lunch.

MICHAEL: Is it from Dot? Who are you?

JEE: Dot?

MICHAEL: Is it…did Dot give it to you? *(Beat.)* Who gave… just a minute. *(Goes back to the phone.)*

JEE: Wow. This is some view from up here. What flo –

ZOO: 73rd.

JEE: Wow. You can see everything. How long would it take to fall from, like, the 73rd floor?

MICHAEL: Long time.

ZOO: I don't think so.

JEE: You busy, Mr. D?

MICHAEL: Yeah…I'm…

ZOO: Well, we brought you your lunch.

MICHAEL: *(He's off the phone.)* Look, guys…

ZOO: We'll just leave it under your desk.

JEE: Sure is a nice view from up here. Man, I would love to have an office with a view from up here.

ZOO: I wouldn't.

JEE: Why not?

ZOO: Too high up.

MICHAEL: What do you boys want?

ZOO: Nothing.

MICHAEL: Why didn't Dot bring my lunch?

JEE: She wanted us to.

MICHAEL: Why?

JEE: I don't know. Oh. You got a minute?

MICHAEL: No, I –

ZOO: We'll show you.

JEE: Yeah. It'll just take a second.

> *Lighting change. They leave one area to enter a 2nd lit area. DOT meets them. They are not dancing. The music and flashing lights are gone.*

ZOO: Dot! Dot! Look what I made. *(He is holding the lunch out for DOT.)*

JEE: Zoo's a fuckin genius.

DOT: What is it?

JEE: It's your dad's "lunch".

> *DOT takes the lunch and looks in it.*

DOT: Wow.

ZOO: It's for your dad.

DOT: Oh my God.

JEE: I know.

ZOO: You said you wanted to fuck him up a little.

JEE: Zoo made that.

ZOO: It was super easy.

JEE: If you're Zoo.

ZOO: So you just take it to your dad. Like you're going to have lunch with him. Like you said. You like it?

DOT: This is going to be awesome. Man I am so going to kick my physics project's ass!

Lighting change. The boys return to MICHAEL without the lunch. The music and lights kick back in. They dance. DOT, unlit, does not move and is holding the lunch.

MICHAEL: So Dot has my lunch?

JEE: No, we do.

MICHAEL: But she just –

JEE: Oh. Wait. We'll show you.

Lighting change. ZOO and JEE go back to the earlier scene with DOT, not dancing.

DOT: Uh…I need you guys to take it to him. *(She hands back the lunch.)*

ZOO: Kay.

JEE: I thought you wanted to have lunch with him.

DOT: Yeah. I can't.

JEE: Why not?

DOT: It's a natural law. The principle of familial dynamics.

ZOO: Familial dy – ?

DOT: He's my dad. I'll feel too shitty blowing him up myself. That's what you guys are for. Why do you think I brought you into this project? Don't worry. You're in my bibliography.

She kisses them both on the cheek. DOT's gone. The boys are back with MICHAEL, dancing again as they chat.

MICHAEL: That's not a lunch, is it?

ZOO: Oh yeah. Yeah it's a lunch. *(Pause.)* No. Not really.

MICHAEL: Guys. I've…I've just started a deal that's going to get me moved upstairs.

JEE: Do we have to go back and show you?

MICHAEL: No! No, that's fine.

ZOO: So someone will be calling you. That's how it explodes.

JEE: Yeah, she would have brought the bomb herself but there's some principal of familiar –

ZOO: No, no. Dynamical…?

JEE: Anyway, she didn't want to give you the bomb.

MICHAEL: What if I just throw it out the window?

JEE: Oh I wouldn't pick it up. Right, Zoo?

ZOO: Noooo. Not a good idea.

MICHAEL: What if I leave? Or don't answer?

JEE: And miss the deal with Bill? Not going to happen. *(Both ZOO and JEE laugh.)*

MICHAEL: Why would Dot want to do this to me?

JEE: Dude.

ZOO: Oh my God.

MICHAEL: What.

JEE: Isn't it fuckin obvious? I mean, look at you.

MICHAEL: And you're doing this cause Dot asked you to?

JEE: Well, that, and political reasons.

MICHAEL: Political?

JEE: Yeah.

MICHAEL: What possible political…

JEE: Just look at me, bitch. We're oppressed!

MICHAEL: Oppressed?

ZOO: Hell yeah, fucker!

MICHAEL: How the hell are –

JEE: God, white people think they know everything.

ZOO: Fucking white people.

JEE: Just name something, bitch…

Remember, the boys have been dancing through this. Over the course of this speech, the music slowly fades and the boys gradually stop dancing. By the end they are simply standing with no music.

…My grandparents grew up in post-colonial butt-swamp. In a village the size of my brown thumb with borrowed land from a man who demanded my mom's niece as partial payment to be allowed to suck a few dirty potatoes out of some sad, yellow soil. Name something, bitch. For being confused for an Arab Muslim so often that I decide to pretend to be one of them just to fuck people up. Like the 80 people on the bus who cringe up at me while I playfully fiddle with my backpack. Name something. The fact that I have more in common with white boy Jason, the football quarterback from the suburbs doesn't seem to matter to the cop on the subway who stares at me sideways and is ready to shoot me in the face if I so much as trip over my feet. Like what the fuck is up with the colour of THIS! *(He pulls on a piece of his skin from his cheek and holds it.)* Cause, you know what? My friends don't give a shit! No one I know and love gives a shit. So why do you? Why does the world give a fuckin shit?? Bitch, for being descended from a place so pathetic that people move into the city with the zealous knowledge that whoring your children out is a lucrative option, a step up. And you know what, Mr. D? the wonder of it all is that there's always someone to blame. I can be absolved for hitting my kids, gang raping the villagers, shooting every boy over 13, launching a rocket from Heaven and destroying a neighbourhood to kill ONE FUCKIN GUY!…no matter how stupid I get, there's always someone bigger, better, higher, stupider than me I can blame. And you keep blaming the next guy and the next guy and the next until we find you. Up here on the 73rd floor. Cause there's not much above this, right? I mean above this is like…God, right? And who's gonna blame fucking God? That's the beauty about God. That why God's so perfect. He's always on your side. DO YOU GET IT MR. D? THAT'S WHY I'M SO FUCKING ANGRY!

JEE catches his breath. A stunned moment where MICHAEL does not know what to say.

MICHAEL: I'm…I'm…I really…

JEE and ZOO look at each other. They burst into laughter.

JEE: I'm just fuckin with you!

The music starts up again. So does the boys' dancing.

MICHAEL: What?

JEE: I'm just kiddin, man. I don't give a shit. I live in Cedar View Meadows Estates. We got gates and everything. My parents own, like four strip malls.

ZOO is laughing his ass off.

MICHAEL: *(To ZOO.)* And what's your excuse?

ZOO: What? I don't know. Boys take my lunch money?

ZOO steps forward.

Uh…*(He shouts.)* One!!

The lights change. DOT comes rushing out. MICHAEL and JEE disappear for a moment.

DOT: Who said "one"? It's not one yet! Zoo! What the fuck are you doing?

ZOO: Sorry. I'm…I was…I need to talk to you.

DOT: It's not "one" yet. We're not at one second yet, ok?

ZOO: Yeah, but –

DOT: This is my experiment. I say what second we're at.

ZOO: Yeah, see I don't think –

DOT: I mean you can't just come in and…and change stuff.

ZOO: I know it's just – some shit's not making sense.

DOT: What are you talking about?

ZOO: I'm trying to understand what you're doing.

DOT: What do you mean?

ZOO: Your question.

71

DOT: My question.

ZOO: Yeah, your, like, experimental question.

DOT: What the fuck, Zoo? I – I just want things to be different.

ZOO: Different?

DOT: Yeah. You know, if they changed. Like my family became a real family or something. All in love and happy and shit.

ZOO: That's it?

DOT: Yeah. That's a lot.

ZOO: You're doing this so they'll love you?

DOT: What's wrong with that?

ZOO: Nothing.

DOT: What, Zoo?

ZOO: You need to change your question.

DOT: Why would I need to –

ZOO: You know nothing's going to happen to your dad. He's going to be the same dad doing his dad deals cause that's all you want. You're really not interested in fucking shit up.

DOT: Sure I am. Look at me. I'm fucking shit up like crazy!

ZOO: I think you're ignoring stuff.

DOT: Like what?

ZOO: You have to consider everything if you're going –

DOT: Fuuuuuck! I know! I know. I just. I didn't know things were going to get so complicated, Zooey.

She's getting emotional. She moves closer to ZOO.

ZOO: Yeah. No. I get it. It's all good. I'm sorry if –

DOT: I should be listening to you more. You're so smart and nice.

A big overlap starts.

ZOO: Ok. Yeah. Well I want to help / your…if…like –

DOT: I would. Totally. Yeah / I would love to…if you, like –

ZOO: And I wanted to like…you're…I think you're pretty, / you're pretty hot and –

DOT: So you'll like, help me? With my question and variables and all the D equals D over T shit?

ZOO: Oh yeah. Sure. For sure. But I'm going to be a pretty major variable.

DOT: Ok. Ok. Sure. That's. Sure. No problem.

ZOO: Dot, I think you're pretty awesome / and I was wondering –

DOT: You're awesome too, Zoo. Zoo, have you hooked up with Ming yet?

ZOO: What? No, I –

DOT: She really wants to party with you. Really.

ZOO: Yeah.

DOT: You'll do that for me, right?

ZOO: Yeah.

DOT: Awesome. You're the best. *(She abandons him. ZOO watches her go.)*

We are back to JEE, ZOO, and MICHAEL.

JEE: *(To MICHAEL.)* So we'll leave your lunch right here.

JEE tosses it on the floor.

ZOO: Don't worry, Mr. D. There's only one phone in the whole world that can make it go off.

JEE: Yeah. So don't worry. Oh, this is for you too.

The two pull their pants down and moon MICHAEL laughing the whole time. ZOO pulls his pants up and exits. GEE delays slightly. Lights out on MICHAEL. A change in light, in tone. The techno music stops. LAURA steps in with JEE. She is in her bra. She slowly puts her top back on. JEE has stood up and is slowly pulling his pants up and buckling his belt. It's an obvious post-coital moment. DOT enters to see this. LAURA finishes getting dressed and looks at JEE for a moment then across the stage at her daughter who is just standing, looking. JEE exits.

DOT: Is that my boyfriend you're fucking?

LAURA: No.

DOT: You're not fucking my boyfriend?

LAURA: He's not your boyfriend. You said it yourself he's not.

LAURA does not respond and begins to walk off. DOT shouts off.

DOT: If you think this is going to make me hate you, you're wrong. *(Beat.)* And I know you love me! *(Pause, quietly.)* Bitch.

She stands there at a slight loss and then turns to go off but MING has rolled the bed in and sits on it. MING holds a Teddy Bear. She has lost considerable energy.

MING: …Around the corner, under the stairs. You know, by the bathrooms.

DOT: Yeah.

Pause.

MING: It was pretty dark.

DOT: That's where I did it the first time.

MING: I know. You told me. He thought it would be a good place. *(Pause.)* Anyway. My mom thinks we went to a movie.

DOT: We?

MING: You and me.

DOT: Oh. Ok.

Pause.

MING: It tastes gross.

DOT: You don't have to taste it.

MING: I didn't know. *(Pause.)* He kept taking my head and pushing it forward. *(MING demonstrates on herself.)* And talking to me.

DOT: Talking to you?

MING: Yeah like…saying things.

Pause.

My mom's probably here.

MING gets off the bed and rolls it off. DOT watches her go.

DOT: I'll call you, kay?

She waits for a reply that doesn't come.

Shit. *(DOT gives a look to her audience.)* I really didn't… When people have sex in a cartoon, do they really have sex? I mean, I know they don't really. But like, no consequences? Are their bodies or hearts wrecked or something?

Pause.

I'm already tired of sex. And I'm 15.

ZOO appears at a distance.

DOT: Zoo. What did you –

ZOO comes further into the light. He opens his jacket to reveal a vest covered with paper bag lunches like DOT's.

DOT: What are you –

ZOO: See?

Pause. DOT is trying to make sense of this.

DOT: You want to blow up those lunches?

ZOO: Yeah.

DOT: Why?

ZOO: I don't know. It's a better question.

DOT: Zoo. I think you need to go home now.

ZOO: Dot…

DOT: I'll call you, ok?

ZOO: I'm just saying. If I'm a variable then –

DOT: *(Yelling.)* Go home, Zoo! I'll call you.

A pause. ZOO hesitates and then exits.

DOT: *(Looks at audience.)* He's just joking. It's just a side experiment of his. Like a side question.

She looks around, a little lost.

What's…what are we…?

She sees her mom enter from across the stage.

Oh. Yeah. Ok.

Fucking One!

Lighting change. Swoosh. MICHAEL appears, falling. LAURA approaches in a rush.

LAURA: *(To DOT.)* Where's my phone?

DOT: In a minute. *(DOT starts to look through her bag.)*

LAURA: I want a divorce.

DOT: What she means is she wants your undying, unconditional love and affection or a divorce.

LAURA: Dot please, stay out of this.

DOT: I'm helping.

LAURA: How do we get him down?

MICHAEL: *(MICHAEL is desperate, exhausted and not fully coherent.)* Not now! Bill needs me!

DOT: It's gone, Dad. The deal's gone. It's all gone!

LAURA: Michael, get down from the fucking air right now.

DOT: Oh dear. Language.

LAURA: I'm starting over. I want to start over.

DOT: We are. We are starting over.

MICHAEL: We'll…we'll go to counseling!

DOT/LAURA: No!

LAURA: Have you lost your mind? Look at you. Flailing around in the air. And how the fuck are we supposed to get a divorce when you're…

In frustration, LAURA reaches up and grabs – if he's grabable – at MICHAEL to pull him down.

DOT: You can't dick around with gravity, Mom. That's gravity you know, and gravity will not be dicked around with.

MICHAEL: What are you doing? You trying to kill me?

DOT: Mom, he's already falling as fast as he can. Don't worry. It's going to happen. Gravity is just –

LAURA: Will you shut up with your "gravity"? *(LAURA stops pulling on him.)*

DOT: Come on, Dad. Some last words. I think you're finally starting to see, aren't you Dad? Aren't you?

LAURA: We need to talk about custody.

DOT: Ok. Divorce. Custody! Mom, it's going to be great. We can travel, be best friends. And Dad! We can go to movies, walks in the park.

LAURA: I understand the sacrifices you've made over the years. And I believe some kind of compensation should be awarded when it comes to getting Dot.

DOT: That's fair. How much am I worth to you, Dad?

MICHAEL: Not now! I'm very…busy. I'm making a deal.

DOT: I know. That's why we're here. Let's make a deal.

MICHAEL: No. The deal. The business –

LAURA: …So you can have the boat, which I know you love… if you take Dot.

DOT looks at her mom.

MICHAEL: *(Fighting for breath.)* What?! If I take? I just assumed –

LAURA: No way. A woman cannot make a fresh start with baggage.

MICHAEL: *(Shouting.)* What am I going to do with a 15 year old?

LAURA: The RV. You can have the RV.

MICHAEL: Done!

MICHAEL disappears. LAURA turns to go.

DOT: Mom?

LAURA: Yes, Dot.

DOT: What are you doing?

LAURA: What do you mean?

DOT: I gave you a million chances.

LAURA: You're too little to see it yet, Dotty.

DOT: See what?

LAURA: You don't think it's already started to grab you too?

DOT: What.

LAURA: Your precious gravity.

DOT: Mom, I was trying to rescue us.

LAURA: I don't need your rescuing.

DOT: Not you. Us.

> Oh. You need to call Dad. He has some news about your audition.

DOT produces her mom's phone.

DOT: Sorry. Forgot I had it.

LAURA grabs her phone.

LAURA: About time…

She begins to dial MICHAEL. Music begins to play – tragic, soft, beautiful. Anything from Mozart concerto #21 to some dreamy trip hop.

DOT: And my mom who has been wanting this since the moment she got married, calls my dad on the only phone that can blow up his lunch, and they finally make the connection I've been longing for since I was born.

A light up on MICHAEL.

MICHAEL: Hello? Bill?

A light up on LAURA.

LAURA: Hello? Michael?

Darkness. An explosion and a flash – identical to the one at the beginning. Then the lights come back on DOT.

DOT: And as I watch my dad crescendo through exploding glass from the 73rd floor of his office tower miles and miles in the air, his body launching, tumbling over itself in slow motion, I remember another other law of physics I haven't paid a lot of attention in this, the grandest of all 10th grade science experiments in the history of the world: Every action requires an equal and opposite reaction. Cartoons don't get that. Like, you get the reaction? But not the change. You need the change.

The lights come up to reveal MICHAEL, LAURA, MING, and JEE all falling. It is poetic, beautiful. The music has turned it into a ballet. DOT snaps a photo.

IMAGE #9: Michael, Laura, Jee, Ming falling.

These people need to experience that reaction.

She watches for a moment, smiles.

Only Zoo escapes my physicist wrath.

They continue to fall, the music, beautiful and tragic, continues to play. Six seconds suddenly seems like an eternity.

DOT: Everything falls at the same rate. A belligerent dad, a psychotic mom, an asshole boyfriend, a best friend so exquisite she makes you feel like a whithered, beaten down 19 year old.

Lights go out on The "fallers" and remain only on DOT. The images disappear as well.

They all travel at a marvelous 58.8 meters per second with a force of 940.8 kilogram meters per second squared – otherwise known as Newtons. And then, to put it in Dad's words, they "land".

A thump, squish-type sound – very cartoon-like.

My dad…

Another thump, squish.

My "boyfriend."

A third sound.

My best friend. And finally…

A fourth thump squish – perhaps each one is slightly different sounding.

My mom. On top of my dad.

MICHAEL and LAURA appear in a pool of light laying motionless splayed on the floor. LAURA is partially on top of MICHAEL. MING and JEE are not there.

Zero.

DOT: Their final velocity was 211 kilometers per hour. That is really…fast. Now they've got no velocity, no acceleration, no momentum. It's like starting over again from nothing. And now we can all together witness the final results of my famous experiment.

DOT watches as her parents slowly come to life and stand up. While it seems slightly painful, it shouldn't be anything significant. Perhaps they dust themselves off. They stand there smiling.

DOT: Well…?

LAURA/MICHAEL: Well?

DOT: What did you think?

LAURA: *(They seem the same.)* Oh. My precious, little Dot. That was…that was spectacular.

DOT: Thanks. What did you think of the ending?

MICHAEL: Loved it. Wow. Your mom landing smack on top me. Ka pow! That was something else.

LAURA: Incredible.

MICHAEL: If you don't get an A I'm calling the school.

LAURA: We are so proud.

MICHAEL: We are. We're very very proud.

The parents go to "group hug" DOT. DOT stops them before they can.

DOT: Are we…we're not divorced?

LAURA: What do you mean?

DOT: You're…we're not…divorced?

MICHAEL: Of course not.

LAURA: Now why would we ever do that? We love you too much for that.

DOT: You do?… Really?

MICHAEL: Absolutely.

LAURA: So so much.

DOT: But I just made you fall splat to the ground.

MICHAEL: We did. We really did.

LAURA: And we deserved it.

DOT: Mom, you're not, like, pregnant or anything?

LAURA: Pregnant? Why would I be – Do I look pregnant to you? *(Laughter.)*

MICHAEL: Now I have a great idea. Why don't you go party or something. Go to a party and do some E or something.

DOT: Dad…I'm 15.

MICHAEL: Not for long, pumpkin.

JEE enters wearing a suit jacket identical to MICHAEL's. He's a very different JEE; bright, corporate.

JEE: Hey, Dot.

DOT: Jee, what are you –

MICHAEL: I hired him.

JEE: Your dad hired me. I'm going to be starting off on the 28th floor. Pretty cool, huh? He's going to teach me the ropes so I can take over for my parents sometime.

DOT: Yeah…cool.

MICHAEL: He's got quite a future. He's a serious gangbanger, aren't ya, Jay?

JEE: Jee.

LAURA: Jee is a hardcore gangbanger.

DOT: Aren't you sad about your audition, Mom?

LAURA: Sad? Why would I be sad? It went great! I think I got it.

JEE: Anyways, You coming Dot?

DOT: What? Where?

JEE: We're going to celebrate your birthday. Remember? It's your birthday tomorrow.

MICHAEL: Sweet 16.

LAURA: My God. Sixteen. You take good care of her tonight, Jee.

JEE: I will, Mrs. D.

LAURA: Don't worry. She's on the pill.

MICHAEL: That was a really smart move on your part, honey. / The pills.

LAURA: It just seemed sensible, you know? It really did.

DOT: *(To her parents.)* Get out.

MICHAEL: What?

LAURA: Dot!

DOT: Get out. Leave. Right now.

MICHAEL: Dot, why? We're your parents!

DOT: No. You're not. Get out. Get the fuck out. I'll finish this myself.

She starts pushing them out the exit.

JEE: I'll see ya later Mrs. D. See you at work, Mr. D.

LAURA: Dot, I don't understand.

DOT: What was the point of this whole thing? You're worse! It's stupid! I have no idea how I'm supposed to change anything. The experiment was stupid.

LAURA: Dot don't be that way. We're just being what you want.

DOT: I don't know what I want.

MICHAEL: Of course you don't. You're fifteen.

JEE: Sixteen. Remember?

DOT: *(To audience.)* Tonight at midnight. My friends are going to take me out and make me drink 15 shooters, one for each year I've lived. Makes me wish I was turning 8…or 6 or something.

Her parents are still standing there. DOT looks at them.

DOT: Go.

LAURA: All right! All right!

MICHAEL: Oh. Don't forget. We have to take that big detour away from downtown.

Her parents are exiting. They stop.

LAURA: Oh, right. The explosion.

DOT: Explosion? What explosion?

MING is there. DOT turns to see her. MING looks a lot like DOT now. She has changed into an outfit resembling DOT's. Her pose, her look is very different in tone. There's very little "child" in her. Music plays. It is haunting house-style rhythmic. JEE begins to groove to it; just small moves as MING speaks.

MING: …And some time later, Zoo boarded a city bus, the 102 heading downtown from the suburbs and dropped in his token.

MICHAEL: Somebody blew themselves up on a city bus.

JEE: You coming?

LAURA: …Terrible, just terrible…

MING: …a bus is very contained.

MICHAEL: …Bodies, pieces everywhere…

DOT: No. Ming. That's…I told Zoo –

LAURA: I mean, what motivates someone to do something like that?

DOT: What are you guys talking about? Ming?

JEE: Dot, you coming? *(He continues his slow groove.)*

MING: And he wandered down the aisle and stood in front of an elderly woman clutching a fat, red purse.

LAURA: …Why? Why would anyone do something like that?

MICHAEL: …Awful, really really sad, really…

LAURA: …Terrible. / Just –

DOT: No, see it's not / supposed to be –

MING: Then he reached into his jacket pocket and grasped a handle with a little red switch…

JEE: You coming Dot?

DOT: I told him not –

JEE: Dot, you coming? *(JEE is still dancing.)*

MING: …From those old boxing robots. You know, their heads pop up?

LAURA: Some sort of extremist thing, probably.

MING: …With his mass at about 81 kilograms, Zoo calculated that the force exerted on his body at the time of explosion would be somewhere around 18,630 kilogram meters per second.

JEE: Dot, we gotta go.

DOT does nothing.

DOT: *(Finally, to JEE.)* That's ok. You go without me.

JEE: You sure? *(He stops dancing. Music stops.)*

She doesn't respond. JEE shrugs and splits.

MING: His head and one shoulder separated from his body. His middle pretty much disintegrated. It became a part of everybody else as everything kind of went all over the bus.

Serves him right. Fucking son-of-a-bitch.

DOT: *(To us.)* That wasn't…wasn't part of the…
um, experiment –

MICHAEL: All right. Let's get you home.

DOT: No! You! Both of you! Get out get out get out get out!

Oh. Here's your makeup. I decided I don't want it. *(She hands LAURA the makeup.)*

LAURA: Fine but don't be surprised if the doors are locked when you get home.

DOT: Fine!

LAURA and MICHAEL give her a defiant look and exit. DOT turns to the audience.

DOT: That's not…that wasn't…

She turns to look out into the darkness.

Zoo??? …Zoo what did you…? What…?

There is no response. She turns to MING.

MING: Force equals mass times acceleration. F equals M A. Impulse is F times delta T which is also equal to P which equals momentum.

(To DOT.) See? You taught me well.

MING stands up and looks straight at DOT.

DOT: What.

MING: Nothing. *(Pause.)* I'm going.

DOT: Oh. Ok. You don't want to hang out later?

MING: No.

DOT: Ok. That's ok.

MING exits.

DOT: *(To audience, timidly.)* I think Ming learned a lot today.

ZOO appears from a distance. He looks like a cartoon character who has just had a bomb exploded on him. His clothes are ragged and torn and burnt. His face is full of soot and blood. He stands in the same spot he stood at the beginning of the play. DOT sees him.

DOT: Zoo?

Nothing.

DOT: Zoo, what are you…

…

Zoo?

…

Say something, Zoo.

…

Fucking say something!

ZOO fades into darkness.

DOT stands there for a moment unsure what to do. Then slowly, quietly, the theatre door opens and DOT's parents MICHAEL and LAURA come in. They are quite different from the DOT and LAURA we got to know. They are dressed slightly differently, more drab, perhaps they have coats on. They seem duller, more diminutive, even shy as they walk onto the stage quietly, sheepishly.

DOT: Hi.

MICHAEL: Hi Dot. How'd it go?

DOT: Ok. Good. Good I think.

MICHAEL: Good.

DOT: *(To audience.)* These are my parents.

LAURA and MICHAEL look to the audience and smile pleasantly saying quiet hellos.

DOT: How was your day, Mom?

LAURA: Good…good.

DOT: What about you, Dad?

MICHAEL: Oh, all right I guess. You win some you lose some. You never came to meet me for lunch.

DOT: Sorry. I got busy with my project.

LAURA: And it went well?

DOT: Yeah.

MICHAEL: Sorry we couldn't be there.

DOT: That's…that's ok.

LAURA: All right let's get you home.

They hand DOT her coat and turn to go. DOT holds it but does not put it on.

DOT: I need to go downtown.

LAURA: Downtown? You heard what happened downtown?

DOT: Yeah.

MICHAEL: It's all sealed off. Besides, how are you going to get home?

DOT: I don't know. I'm…going to go downtown.

LAURA: Honey. That's…that's where the explosion was.

DOT: I know.

MICHAEL: You should come home with us. Where it's safe.

DOT: …Safe?

MICHAEL: Yes. Safe, dammit. What the hell would you – you won't be allowed anywhere near the…the site. And what would you do there, anyway?

DOT: Pick up the…pieces. Help people. Tell them I'm sorry.

LAURA: Sorry? Sorry for what?

DOT: Aren't you sorry?

Her parents look at her as though they have no idea what she means.

LAURA: You'll come home with us. Now get your coat on. Let's go. I'm sure you're tired.

There's a slight pause as though DOT is trying to find some way to separate herself from her parents.

DOT: Ok. I'll be right there. Just a couple of things I have to do.

MICHAEL: All right. We'll be…we'll be in the car.

LAURA/MICHAEL: *(Turn to the audience.)* Nice to meet you.

LAURA: Don't be long, sweetie.

DOT: Yeah. Ok. Oh. Dad?

MICHAEL: Yeah, Dot?

DOT: *(Pause.)* In those old cartoons. Does Yosemite Sam ever make Bugs fall?

MICHAEL: Nope. Don't think so. He tries to make Bugs fall but he can't see.

DOT: Can't see what?

MICHAEL: What he's doing. So he's the one who falls. Every time.

A pause. They look at DOT. They're gone. DOT turns back to the audience.

DOT: I hope you learned something today and have a greater understanding of Newtonian physics. You were a good audience except maybe for some shuffling around and coughing and stuff.

…

I'm…I'm gonna go…downtown.

…

Some of you could come with me if you wanted…and… and help.

…

Nobody? Ok. So anyways…bye.

DOT stands there. Beautiful, sweet music begins to play as DOT slowly puts her coat on. On the screen behind and above her we begin to see a video of DOT, falling slowly, beautifully, spectacularly. She is smiling and plunging through the sky. DOT does not see or notice this as she finishes getting ready and slowly out a different way away from her parents.

DOT falls for some time then fades.

The End.

WWW.OBERONBOOKS.COM

Follow us on www.twitter.com/@oberonbooks
& www.facebook.com/oberonbook